Geoff and Cyd Holsclaw integrate brain science and attachment theory with theology to offer us a way to get unstuck in our faith. Their research is clearly deep, broad, and well footnoted, but amazingly, they have written in such a way that we can easily find ourselves in their work. This book is wonderfully practical, offering us a lot not only to think about but also to put into practice. A lot of readers will find tremendous relief and breakthroughs in their faith by engaging this book.

STEVE CUSS, author and host of the *Being Human* podcast

Landscapes of the Soul is a profoundly insightful guide for anyone seeking a deeper understanding of how "attachment" shapes our formation and relationships. Cyd and Geoff Holsclaw weave together the wisdom of neuroscience, theology, and lived experience to offer a vision of transformation that is both deeply practical and profoundly spiritual. As someone who has done some work on healing an attachment wound in my own story, I found the Holsclaws' invitation to attachment theory and the healing power of the love of God to deepen my desire to continue the healing journey. This book is an invaluable resource for cultivating a faith that is securely rooted in God's presence and love.

JARED PATRICK BOYD, founding director of Order of the Common Life

Landscapes of the Soul

TYNDALE
REFRESH™
Think Well. Live Well. Be Well.

LANDSCAPES OF THE SOUL

How the Science and Spirituality of Attachment Can Move You into Confident Faith, Courage, and Connection

Cyd & Geoff Holsclaw

Foreword by Jim Wilder

Visit Tyndale online at tyndale.com.

Tyndale, Tyndale's quill logo, *Tyndale Refresh*, and the Tyndale Refresh logo are registered and/or common law trademarks of Tyndale House Ministries in the USA and various other jurisdictions around the world. All rights reserved. See tyndale.com for a full list of trademarks owned by Tyndale House Ministries.
Tyndale Refresh is a nonfiction imprint of Tyndale House Publishers, Carol Stream, Illinois.

Landscapes of the Soul: How the Science and Spirituality of Attachment Can Move You into Confident Faith, Courage, and Connection

Cover designed by Libby Dykstra

Interior designed by Laura Cruise

Edited by Jonathan Schindler

Published in association with Don Gates of the literary agency The Gates Group; www.the-gates-group.com.

For information about special discounts for bulk purchases, please contact Tyndale House Publishers at csresponse@tyndale.com, or call 1-855-277-9400.

Library of Congress Cataloging-in-Publication Data

A catalog record for this book is available from the Library of Congress.

ISBN 979-8-4005-0554-6

Printed in the United States of America

32 31 30 29 28 27 26
8 7 6 5 4 3 2

To Tennyson, Soren, and Isabelle:
May you each live from your foundation of joyful connection, keep growing in intimacy and independence, and continue to be drawn deeper into the pasture as you follow the Shepherd who calls you by name.

Contents

Foreword

Attachments keep us connected to each other and shape our expectations of feeling loved. When our attachment patterns don't match with others', our expectations aren't met and life becomes deeply painful.

Our attachment to God may also fail to meet our expectations. We often expect that if someone really cares about us, they will keep us from suffering. This expectation is set during infancy. Yet Jesus, who claimed to be loved by God, predicted a different attachment pattern—one that included pain.

In *Landscapes of the Soul*, Cyd and Geoff Holsclaw describe God's way of attachment using the image of living in a pasture. This sounds pleasant, yet we may be shocked to find ourselves there. If we grew up expecting a jungle, desert, or war zone, God's good attachment response may feel distant, rejecting, or unloving. Do we know what to expect from the pasture attachment style?

Geoff and Cyd base their four landscapes (Jungle, Desert, War Zone, Pasture) on the four well-researched attachment patterns that develop in infants. These four patterns are widely distributed across the world's families and cultures. Each pattern develops by our adapting to the conditions of our young lives and forms the expectations that we carry with us—even when we move to a new landscape.

Yet for all our differences, God desires to attach to all of us. God's people are instructed to glue (*dabaq*) themselves to God four times in Deuteronomy. In the New Testament, Paul commands that we glue (*kollao*) ourselves to "what is good" in Romans 12:9. Have you ever been told how you glue yourself to God?

The transition into the Pasture is different depending on what we learned from our early landscapes. For every one of the three fear-based attachment patterns, *Landscapes of the Soul* shows us what it will take to glue ourselves to God.

Green pastures are high in joy, intimacy, independence, faith, hope and love. That all sounds wonderful. But strong attachments also pass through the valley of the shadow of death. In the Pasture we learn to face pain and fear no evil. We learn comfort while dying with Jesus and through many other strange experiences that can make us feel unloved if we don't know how this new kind of "glue" will hold us close to God. The Holsclaws show us what to expect as we grow in our attachment to God.

Little children are formed by attaching to the sources of life. Jesus told us that everyone who enters the Kingdom of God must enter as a little child. This requires a huge change. The child in everyone needs a new attachment. Find your path with Cyd and Geoff in *Landscapes of the Soul.*

Jim Wilder, PhD
Author, speaker, and neurotheologian at Life Model Works

Preface

We all get stuck in our spiritual lives eventually. Maybe we fall into a rut right away, and only much later do we realize it has always been holding us back. Or maybe we grow and mature for a while, but then everything stops. Or maybe a tragedy or a crisis sets us back in a way we didn't feel possible. Too often we've seen people prescribe one-size-fits-all approaches when we get spiritually stuck.

- *Everyone needs to practice spiritual disciplines.*
- *Everyone needs to study and memorize Scripture.*
- *Everyone needs to serve in the community.*
- *Everyone needs to worship and pray more.*
- *Everyone needs to become an activist.*
- *Everyone needs to become a mystic.*

As local church pastors for over twenty years and over ten as spiritual director and coach (Cyd) and seminary professor (Geoff), we've known one-size-fits-all approaches don't work. What also doesn't work is trying a little bit of everything. What inevitably happens is people gravitate to what they like best, or what works best for them, and then create their own personalized approach and find other people who feel the same way. To some extent, this is a great solution! However, focusing on what feels good or seems to work for them individually keeps them comfortably lounging in the shallow end of the pool. When tragedy or crisis comes, they find that life in the shallows can't accommodate the tidal wave.

Something deeper needed to be addressed.

What we eventually found, and what we share in this book, is that spiritual pathways are connected to our relational and neural pathways, and these are shaped by our attachment relationships. These attachment relationships shape—in the deepest possible way—the strategies we use to navigate our relationships with God, with others, and with ourselves.[1]

Over the last seventy years, attachment research has slowly discovered how our relational attachments form, why some are better than others (called secure and insecure attachment), how four different approaches to relationships emerge from our early attachments, and how we carry these different strategies into adult relationships, and even our relationship with God.[2]

These four different attachment strategies—which we call the Jungle of Anxiety, the Desert of Avoidance, the War Zone of Chaos, and the Pasture of Joy and Peace—are why one-size-fits-all approaches to spiritual formation don't work.

But as you will see, we do not need entirely different practices or pathways for the different attachment strategies. Instead, the goal is to understand how each attachment strategy might use (or abuse) the more well-known practices and pathways, and then allow God to meet us in our insecure attachment strategy and move us deeper into secure attachment.

Unlike other psychological theories or personality profiles, we were drawn to attachment theory because it so clearly connects with the story of God's love in the Bible. We mapped out this story in our first book, *Does God Really Like Me?: Discovering the God Who Wants to Be with Us*, which moved from Genesis to Revelation to show what it means that God delights in us. In this book, we will go even deeper, beyond how we can learn to delight in the God who delights in us to how we can become deeply attached to the God who is deeply attached to us.

CHAPTER 1

SURVIVING TRAUMA & HOPING FOR CHANGE

Imagine being dropped on a small jungle island. Your skills, habits, and instincts for surviving would quickly be tailored to that specific environment. Whatever tools or habits didn't help you survive would be discarded.

Or think of being dropped in the middle of a desert. To survive, you would develop skills, habits, and instincts totally different from what you would need in the jungle.

All of us—through the twists and turns of our particular lives and because of sin in the world—find ourselves in different landscapes. While one person believes life is a jungle, another person lives as if it's a desert. Someone else lives like it's a war zone, while another lives as if it's a lush, green meadow. These landscapes feel like home because they are all we've ever known. And we have developed survival skills adapted to the landscape we live in and from.

Throughout this book, we will use the scientific research on attachment theory to look at how you actually *were* dropped into a jungle, desert, war zone, or pasture at birth and how you learned to survive in that environment by gaining skills suited for that attachment landscape. And we will look at how these landscapes have shaped your faith—how you pray, worship, and read the Bible. It has shaped your expectations of churches you have attended and how you relate to other Christians. Your attachment landscape has even shaped your view of God.

But you aren't meant to live as if life were a jungle, a desert, or a war zone. You aren't meant to live in anxiety, avoidance, or chaos. God designed you to live in joy and peace, as if you were in a pasture, under the protective care of the Good Shepherd.

The good news is that no matter which landscape you find yourself living in, Jesus meets you where you are, and he can also help you move toward the life of joy and peace you are made to live—a life deeply attached to God.

To show you this good news, we'll spend some time talking about the way God designed you to live (Part 1: Good Roots), how your early relationships can distort this design (Part 2: Gone Wrong), and how we can become deeply attached to God throughout it all (Part 3: God's Repair).

This isn't a parenting book or a relationship book. This book is about attaching to God, following Jesus, and growing in the joy and peace of the Spirit. It's a book about how you wound up where you find yourself. And it's a book about how you don't have to stay there.

So let's dive in.

He Must Be Dead

He must be dead, I (Cyd) was thinking. Just like my father died suddenly. Just like my mother died suddenly. Now Geoff was dead. He must be.

In the lobby, I was trying desperately to keep it together in front of the security guard. But my heart was racing. I couldn't breathe. Tears were welling up in my eyes. And my entire body was tense. I was bracing for impact. Geoff was thirty minutes late picking me up from work. The only explanation was that he was dead.

For the first ten minutes, I kept it cool on the outside, but I was already planning his funeral, making important decisions for my future, and steeling myself for life as a widow.

Then the what-if game started. *What if there's something I could be doing to keep him alive? What if he's stuck in a crumpled car and needs medical attention? What if he's passed out in the middle of the toothpaste aisle? What if he's being held at gunpoint at the gas station? What if . . . ?* (This was before cell phones.)

After twenty minutes, I was pacing the lobby like a caged tiger. My sympathetic nervous system was kicking in—fighting and fleeing within myself.

This is ridiculous. He's fine.

Can I get a refund on his tuition? Can I sublet our apartment?

Good grief, pull it together. He's only a few minutes late.

I'm definitely quitting this job—I hate it. I'll go back to California and start over.

Stop freaking out! Stop being a crazy woman!

Oh God, don't let him be dead. Do something! Please!

By this point, total collapse was threatening. My sympathetic nervous system started giving up because there was no one to fight and nowhere to flee. My parasympathetic nervous system was taking over, trying to conserve what little energy I had by shutting down my systems.

I was avoiding eye contact with the people coming and going through the lobby. Feeling so alone. Wanting to cry. Wanting to be held, to get away, to curl up in a ball. *If after four months of marriage he's dead, then what's the point? Will every person I ever love die suddenly?*

Then our little red Subaru hatchback pulled into the parking lot. I got in and burst into tears. Geoff—having driven to the wrong building across town and then gotten stuck in Chicago traffic—had no idea what was wrong.

You might be reading this and thinking, *She really* is *crazy*. But there's a good reason I was flipping out. It all made sense within the story of my life, a story that literally shaped my body's nervous system and the thoughts in my brain.

My father was killed in a car accident when I was fifteen months old. I was in the car. And when I was twenty-six years old, my mom died suddenly from a brain aneurysm. I found her on the bathroom floor.

These pivotal moments still lived in my body, even if I wasn't consciously aware of them. And every time I got anywhere close to the possibility of death, these adrenaline-filled moments returned to my body and clouded my brain, all without my conscious choice or understanding.

Every time someone in my life wasn't where they said they would be, I assumed they were dead. Not late. Not stuck in traffic. Dead.

It Only Takes Once

It takes a long time to learn cognitive information and practical skills. That's why you spend so much time in school learning math, history, reading, and writing. That's why you have to practice so long before getting your driver's license. It takes a lot of brain power to store and then recall facts and figures, skills, and techniques.

Relational and emotional learning, however, is faster. From earliest childhood, you are constantly watching and interacting with people, picking up everything like a sponge. You need fewer positive (or negative) emotional experiences before your brain and body remember and recall those interactions, using past experiences as a guide for future expectations.

But fear or trauma learning, especially when connected to key relationships, is the fastest of all. It only takes one event, one experience, one tragic accident, or one act of abuse for your body and brain to learn the lesson.[1]

Below conscious thought and awareness, you have learned the new "reality." Thought or unthought, it sounds like . . .

- *I won't ever do that again.*
- *It's always my fault.*
- *I'm never going to tell anyone about that.*

- *I guess I'm helpless in these situations.*
- *I have no choice.*
- *I have no voice.*

The younger you are when these accidents, traumas, or abuses happen, the less you are able to think about the promises you've made to yourself, the hopes you've given up on, or the fears you've internalized. It might take years or decades to realize the lessons you've learned.

And what you've learned—what we all learn—is how to survive.

Survival Skills

We are all trying to survive. And surviving takes skill, especially when you are alone in the wilderness, with winter coming, and you are trying to win a million dollars.

Alone, a survival reality show, drops ten people off in the middle of nowhere. The "game" is to see how long contestants can last finding their own food, making their own shelter, and enduring the bitter elements. Each contestant gets to choose ten pieces of gear to bring with them (out of forty possible items). With these minimal tools, they have to hunt and gather food; protect that food from animals; and stay warm, dry, and hydrated for as long as they can, until they either tap out or are removed under medical advisement. The last one to survive wins.

Along with their physical tools, each contestant comes with a vast knowledge about where to find food, different ways of starting a fire, how to build a durable shelter, and anything else they've learned about surviving in the wilderness. All these survival skills are necessary if they want to be the last contestant standing—or, really, the last one shivering and hungry.

You are the same.

You have survival skills—relational and emotional survival skills you learned as a child. Skills that helped you when you needed protection. Abilities that helped you when you needed connection. Maybe your survival skills are focused on how to read people, understanding how they are doing and what they need. Or your survival skills are focused on problem-solving, understanding patterns and following rules. All of us have relational and emotional survival skills that developed within a particular relational and emotional environment.

Over time, these survival skills grow into attachment strategies. These attachment strategies are the regular use of specific survival skills to navigate the relational and emotional environment you live in (you'll learn specifically about these attachment strategies in part 2).[2]

Most of the time you're not thinking about your survival skills or attachment strategies. You're just using them. When you're distressed, threatened, or overwhelmed, they activate. And you don't usually know or think about it. Your survival skills and attachment strategies automatically shape your view and experience of other people, God, the world, and yourself.

And a big part of your relational reality is how you shift between *connection* and *protection.*

Connection or Protection

In our first months of marriage, Cyd and I (Geoff) were cruising down the highway, headed to Chicago. We were sharing favorite songs, talking about life, and enjoying each other's presence. Our focus was on the conversation and the music. We were connecting about the little things and the big dreams of life. Miles flew by without a thought about actually driving the car.

But then—and this regularly happens in the Midwest—we drove right into a heavy rainstorm, the likes of which I had never seen before because I was raised in California. The water rushed off the windshield between the wiper blades as visibility decreased to almost nothing. I turned the headlights on, slowed way down, and turned the radio off. We stopped talking. I needed to concentrate on driving.

Because of the storm, my focus shifted from connection to protection. My connection skills of listening and talking turned off, and my protection skills—in this case, the ability to drive through a storm—turned on.

Switching from connection to protection happens the same way in your body and brain because of your autonomic nervous system (ANS). The sympathetic and parasympathetic systems (which Cyd was moving through when she thought Geoff was dead) are part of the ANS. Your ANS keeps your lungs breathing, heart beating, stomach digesting (and a bunch of other things). This all happens without your conscious awareness. When your ANS senses that life is safe and manageable, it focuses on connecting with others. When your ANS senses a physical or relational storm, it focuses on protecting you.[3] Your nervous system does one or the other very efficiently, but it doesn't do both at the same time. When you're focused on connecting, you don't feel a need to protect. When you switch to protecting, it's very difficult to connect.

It is God's good design that you shift between connection and protection. Your nervous system was made to scan your environment, focus on what is happening inside and outside you, and decide whether it's safe to connect or whether you need to protect yourself.

When Cyd was leaving work and talking with coworkers, she felt safe. Her ANS did not detect any dangers inside or outside her, so she prioritized connection. She chatted with the security guard, thought about what she would make for dinner, and was looking forward to seeing Geoff. Because her nervous system didn't detect any danger, she was able to be calm and relational.

But once a few minutes had gone by and Geoff had not arrived, Cyd's ANS detected danger and flipped into protection mode. She was reacting from a place of survival, moving between the more active sympathetic system (fight-or-flight) and the more passive parasympathetic system (rest and digest). Because her survival mode had been formed through the childhood death of her father and recently reinforced by the death of her mother, Cyd started bracing for another death.

Now here's the twist.

All of us flow between connection and protection in different ways and for different reasons. Why? Because we have lived through different experiences (some traumatic) and in different relational and emotional environments. How we were raised, the specific survival skills we've learned, and the attachment strategies we've developed all impact how we respond to the common storms of life.

Yes. Maybe. No.

Let's shift from how our nervous system works to how it became wired to react the way it does. Much of your life—your life with God, with others, and with yourself—boils down to one of these three words: *yes, maybe, no.*[4]

Your specific survival skills, your attachment strategies, and your relational hopes and dreams emerge from this yes, maybe, or no.

Of course, you don't consciously know this—you were a baby when these words began shaping your life. You don't realize how these words control your movement between connection and protection. But they do.

Yes, maybe, or no are the three possible answers to one simple question: *If I'm in distress, will someone help me?*

- *Yes. Someone* will *help me.*
- *Maybe. Someone* might *help me.*
- *No. Someone* will not *help me.*

One of these three words has been

- defining your relationships,
- influencing your emotions,
- shaping your experience of your body, and
- directing the flow of your thoughts.

One of these three words—*yes*, *maybe*, *no*—has been forming the very development and function of your brain, the structuring of your nervous system, and how you experience connection or perceive the need for protection. One of these three words has become your default expectation when it comes to relationships. (We will learn more about these attachment defaults in chapter 4.)

Sometimes you are completely accurate in understanding that certain people are not trustworthy. They really aren't dependable and are not for you. But other times you're making assumptions about someone's availability without knowing it and never giving them the chance to prove otherwise. It's because of your default of yes, maybe, or no.

Thankfully, as you will see, you can change your answer. Or rather, by becoming securely attached to God, your answer will change. And this will change everything in your life. The yes, maybe, or no that you live from is not your personality type. It is the strategy you used to protect yourself and survive. And God wants more for you than to just survive. God wants you to thrive!

But how does this change happen?

The Problem with Problems

Websites, ads, magazines, and books—even books like this one—often utilize the same pattern: Identify a problem, offer a simple solution, then show how life will get better. Are you tired of spending all your time shopping and cooking? Get your groceries mailed to you with recipes. Then you'll have more time for the things you love. Problem, solution, better life. It's the way of marketing. And it's effective. It sells.

Simple Problem ▶ *Speedy Solution* ▶ *Superficial New Life*

You might be reading this book because of this formula. Maybe you picked it up because you feel stuck, like something is wrong or broken about your ability to connect with God or others. Maybe you worry that you have an anxious or an avoidant faith, and you want to fix it. Or you just learned that you have attachment strategies living below your consciousness and they are influencing almost every choice you make. Now you *definitely* want to fix it.

That's not a bad thing. But your brain isn't very open to change when it is focused on problems. When you are focused on getting rid of a problem, your stress level goes up, your cognitive function goes down, and you lose your curiosity and creativity. Starting with the problem puts you into protection mode.

Recently, I (Cyd) decided I wanted to learn how to play worship music on the piano. I already knew how to read music because of many years of classical training in piano and clarinet. I am especially strong in sight reading but not great at improvising with just the chords in mind. However, Geoff has played the guitar since high school and thinks in chord structures. My brain doesn't seem to work that way.

As I tried to learn, I got frustrated. I could easily articulate my problem: "I can't think in chords because I'm so used to reading the notes on a page."

I stumbled across a worship piano program online. For one low price, I could learn chord progressions in every key and learn to apply them to worship music to sound like a pro. I bought it. It seemed like the right solution.

- **Problem:** I can't think in chords to play worship piano.
- **Solution:** I'll buy a step-by-step course to relearn chords and apply them to worship songs.
- **Better Life:** I can improvise on the piano based on the chords.

I diligently watched the videos and reviewed my music theory and chord structures. Then the first worship song was introduced with just the chord names written above the lyrics. It was like a wall went up in my brain. I couldn't make the connection between the chords I had just seen written out and the simple letters now sitting above the song lyrics. I still hadn't made the connection to translate the chord names into rhythmic movements for the melody to float on. I was still stuck and wanted to give up.

This selling of transformation—moving from problem to solution—often falls into one of two traps (sometimes both). The first trap is thinking that more information will change us. If we can learn more about the problem, or discover the perfect solution, then things will change (our diet, our relationships, our parenting, our career, etc.).

This is what we try to do when we buy a program to teach us something. We buy information to solve our problem. Sometimes the information changes things for a little while—until it gets hard or complicated. Then we go looking for "better" information to solve the same problem. We try that for a bit before changing again—and on and on it goes.

The second trap is relying on our willpower to implement the solution. Our culture loves willpower, hard work, and bootstrapping. We just need to try harder and do better. This was Geoff's initial solution to Cyd's problem on the piano: "You just need to practice more," he would say, "and then you will get it." The trouble is that relying on willpower rarely lasts.

Science shows that true transformation doesn't come from fixing problems through information and willpower. Lasting transformation comes from a vision of life that is so compelling, it is impossible to stay where we are. From that compelling vision, we start to see the real problem and have the desire to implement a lasting solution.[5]

Vision of a New Life ▶ *The Real Problem* ▶ *Lasting Solution*

Let's get back to the piano problem. I spent some time digging into these questions: *Why is playing worship piano important to me?*

What difference would it make to be able to sit down and play worship songs? I discovered that at bottom was a desire to connect with God in worship. I just wanted to pour out my heart like Geoff could when he played guitar by himself in his office. The deep desire was not to play for others or to help out on Sundays. It was just to worship at home.

Once I discovered my vision of a new life, Geoff surprised me with some easy worship piano books that included all the written notes and chord names. Now I could sit down and read the sheet music—something that was already easy for me—and just connect with God.

Instead of solving a surface problem with an impractical solution for a life you might not really want, we want to offer you a vision of the life God has always wanted to give you, name the problems that keep you from this life, and end by looking at spiritually sensitive and science-backed solutions.

God's Good Design

Rather than beginning with all the struggles you have right now—your fears or frustrations, your doubts or disappointments, your anxieties or avoidances—we are going to explore how God designed you to be securely attached to God and to others.

What would it be like to be so deeply rooted in God that you are full of faith, hope, and love? Full of faith in God being available to you. Full of hope for a better world. And full of love overflowing to others. How would everything be different if you could connect with people in healthy relationships without regularly slipping into protection mode? How would it be to freely offer yourself and your gifts to the communities where you belong and the people you love?

This is the way God designed it to be. God designed your brain and your body to be deeply attached to God and to others. Once you have a vision of how these deep roots are designed to help you thrive (part 1), you can understand how your attachment goes wrong (part 2) and see how God is repairing it all (part 3).

Reflection

*For each of the chapters in part 1, we will offer a few reflection questions to help you pull out the ideas from each chapter (**cognitive**), respond to those ideas (**affective**), and connect those ideas with your **faith**. We encourage you to engage the questions from all three categories.*

COGNITIVE

What stands out to you from the explanation of social-emotional learning, trauma, or your connect/protect priority in your autonomic nervous system?

What feels clearer to you after reading this? What do you find confusing?

What feels like confirmation of your own experience? Where do you feel challenged or in conflict with an idea?

AFFECTIVE

What did you notice feeling as you read about survival strategies? (Search online for "feelings wheel" to help put words to what you're feeling.[6])

How did your body respond to what you read? Did you feel yourself slipping into protection mode? If so, what were you reading when you did?

Did anything you read bring you calm and connection? What was it?

FAITH

How do these understandings of survival and protection connect with your experience of God and of following Jesus?

What sounded like good news to you?

If you were to have a conversation about this chapter with Jesus (or another member of the Trinity—God the Father or God the Holy Spirit), what would you want to talk about?

PART 1

GOOD ROOTS: DESIGNED TO ATTACH

CHAPTER 2

ONE DESIRE: JOYFUL CONNECTION

We have two sons, Soren and Tennyson. They are both in their early twenties now. Born only seventeen months apart, they have always been close, in age and friendship. When they were apart for any amount of time, especially when they were young, they were always quick to reconnect.

Back in the day, we enrolled Soren in a half-day camp for preschoolers. At the end of each day, the children's parents and siblings would spread along the pathway outside the environmental education center. Then the four-year-olds would come out the door with their little backpacks, crafts in hand. And they began searching the crowd for the faces of their people.

Every day, Tennyson would spot his big brother coming down the path. His face would light up and he would shout, "Soren!" and run to him and hug him. Soren's face would light up seeing his little brother, wanting to show Tennyson what he had made and glad for them to be together again. As parents, we beamed with delight seeing the joy shared between them. And when Soren saw our shining faces, he couldn't help but smile back, making us smile even more.

All of us, like Soren, are looking at faces, scanning their response to us, searching for clues. And whether we consciously know it or not, we are hoping to see a face full of joy.

Just imagine seeing the face of a friend after a long absence. Imagine unexpectedly seeing a good friend when you are in an unfamiliar place. Imagine seeing a familiar face when you feel like a stranger at a party. It makes you feel good, relaxed, like you belong. Underneath our desires, we are all looking for joyful connection.

Joy: An Emotion like No Other

Soren experienced joy because Tennyson was excited to see him. As parents, we experienced joy watching the joy between them. And both boys experienced joy in seeing our delight in their reunion.

This is joyful connection.

But what is joy, exactly?

Joy is a relational emotion. It's different from happiness. You can be happy all by yourself, based on circumstances. But joy needs another person—even if it is only the memory of another person. Joy is a relational experience of sharing gladness to be with another person. When you are with someone who wants to be with you, it brings you joy.[1]

Surprisingly, joy can even live next to sadness.

A few years ago, I (Cyd) was at the vet with one of our cats, June. It was clear that she was suffering and it was time to let her go. I had gone by myself, not realizing that this would be her end. The vet asked me, "Is there anyone you would like to call? We can wait if you would like someone to be here with you."

I was so grateful for her thoughtfulness.

Geoff wasn't able to come. He told our two sons, and Soren (now a young man) offered to come, saying, "I don't want Mom to be alone." So we waited until he arrived. Our cat, June, had spent most of her life hiding underneath furniture, and I was the only one who seemed to make her feel safe. No one else in the family had much of a connection with her. Soren came, not because he was so connected to the cat but because he was connected to me.

He didn't want me to be alone. He wanted to be with me. And I was glad he was. Even though I was sad, I was glad because Soren was with me. That's joy, not happiness.

Joy is possible and available even in the middle of difficult circumstances, even during distressing events. If, during times of happiness or sadness, we are surrounded by people we love and who love us, then this is joyful connection. God designed our lives to be grounded in this basic experience of joy from the very beginning of our lives. If things are the way they are intended to be, we are born into joy.

Joyful Connection Required

It is said that the eyes are the windows to the soul. But neuroscience tells us that your entire face is the door to your nervous system.

In the last chapter, we talked about how our nervous system is focused on either connection or protection. Our faces are so expressive because the long bundles of nerves connected to our heart, lungs, and gut are the same ones connected to the muscles surrounding our eyes, ears, and mouth.[2] Your heart beats faster when you lock eyes with a romantic interest. You might feel like your breath is taken away. Or your heart stops when you see a threatening face. Your face is—literally—connected to and communicating with the heart and lungs. This bundle of nerves—the vagus nerve—is the primary way your nervous system shifts between connection and protection. So your face and the faces of others are communicating whether you are feeling connective or protective, and your face can move others in and out of connection and protection.

The muscles of the face are active from birth, unlike the muscles in our arms and legs, which are only partially functional. Researchers have found that just hours after birth, we start looking for the faces and eyes of the people around us. Parents and children regularly "engage in prolonged periods of mutual gazing that calm and relax them both." We are so drawn to the faces of babies that "for most people, the sight of an infant affects them physically and emotionally, drawing them toward the child with increased openness and sensitivity."[3] This is joyful connection.

Joyful connection builds through these face-to-face interactions as joy passes nonverbally from one face to another through eye contact and full-face smiling (which is different from smiling with just the mouth, often called fake smiling). These face-to-face interactions are like exercise routines that expand our capacity for joy. The more repetitions we get, the stronger our joy muscles become. And the bigger our joy muscles grow, the larger our capacity for holding big and complex emotions grows—like feeling sadness and joy at the same time when we had to put down our cat.

These joyful connections form the foundation of attachment—the bond created with those who connect and care for you. Joyful connection is required for a thriving life.

This is the one desire of attachment, to find and grow joyful connection.

We Die Without Joyful Connection

We might think that relieving distress is the most important thing in caring for a baby. This is true for a baby's physical development. But a baby's relational and emotional development comes from interactions of joy that build up the muscles of the nervous system. Without them, a child's growth will be stunted. Withholding the social nutrition of joyful connection is just as damaging as withholding physical nutrition.[4]

In the thirteenth century, Emperor Frederick II conducted an awful experiment to find out what language infants would spontaneously speak if no one spoke to them. He took fifty newborns and allowed them only to be nursed and bathed—their mothers and nurses could not talk or interact with the infants in any other way. These children were left alone with no joyful connection. Emperor Frederick never found out what language they would speak because, tragically, every baby died.[5]

The reality is that as infants, we die when deprived of joyful connection. And as adults, it feels like we are dead on the inside—and we start seeking deadly substitutes—when we are deprived of joyful connection.[6]

For everyone, joyful connection is required.

Our early lives are designed by God to be filled with joyful connections, which come through two different kinds of experiences. The first are interactions that amplify joy. The second are interactions that help us return to joy.

Amplifying Joy—Emotional Caffeine

Imagine you are a baby, less than a year old. You want to connect with the person who brings you joy. You can't talk, and you reserve crying for when you are distressed, so you wiggle around, flap your arms, and kick your legs just enough to get their attention.

When they come over, you give them a big smile. You've learned that if you smile at them, they will smile back at you. And that's when the game begins.

You don't know why, you don't have words for it, but seeing that face smiling at you—and their shining eyes—you start to feel really good inside. And you want more of it.

So you lock eyes with your parent. And thankfully, most parents return the favor and lock eyes with you. Infant research shows that holding eye contact like this does not just keep the positive feelings flowing; it amplifies them, making them grow. This growing feeling is fueling you with joy.[7]

This face-to-face eye contact is like emotional caffeine. It amps you up and gives you energy. It's like slamming a triple shot of espresso. It's like flooring the gas pedal and speeding up.

But eventually, all this emotional energy overwhelms you. You become overstimulated. The good feeling moves from a positive experience to negative distress. Like too much caffeine, you start to feel bad.

So you—the infant—look away. You break eye contact. When you look away, it is like the foot comes off the gas pedal. The caffeine wears off. Your physical and emotional energy level slows down.

The attuned caregiver understands your looking away as the need for a rest. Just a little break to calm down. They respond by resting and waiting to see what you do next. Usually, after a short break, you continue the game of making and holding eye contact, of feeling the good feelings, the game of amplifying joy.

Round and round you go, entering cycles of amplifying joy and then recovering in peaceful rest. Each cycle grows your capacity for higher and higher levels of joyful connection. Each cycle stretches your emotional aptitude. And eventually, you will be able to hold bigger and more intense emotions.

Quite literally, your nervous system is growing and integrating within your brain and your body.

As you grow older, these games of nonverbal eye contact become peekaboo, tug-of-war, and other forms of play. Then they become the desire to show off what you made at school or how well you played in the game. These attempts at amplifying joy continue all the way into adolescence and adulthood. Throughout, your unconscious goal is always the same—to seek out and amplify joyful connection.[8]

Returning to Joy—Emotional Care

But life is not all fun and games.

We volunteer in the children's ministry at our church. There is a toddler who is very much in the process of expanding his world. When mom or dad drops him off for childcare, he struts into the room like he owns the place. He is adventurous and playful and is clearly comfortable in the room. In fact, he's comfortable in the whole church!

Even when he's been picked up, it's not uncommon to see him running around with his older siblings and friends and enjoying himself. But the moment he stumbles or runs into trouble, the first thing he does is look around. If he doesn't immediately see mom or dad, he bursts into tears and starts wandering in search of the faces he knows are available to him.

Because he is well-known in our church and lots of people love him, someone will come and ask him what's wrong. He will whimper out a response, but we all know what he really needs is the comforting face of a parent. So we'll invite him to take our hand, and we assure him, "I'll help you find Mom or Dad." He's immediately a little calmer. Someone is available, and this someone is going to help him find his parents. He knows he's going to be okay.

Once he's reunited with Mom or Dad, he eases into their arms and is comforted. He's connected again and feels the joy of being with the parent who is glad to tend to him.

As a baby, because of your expanding capacity for joyful connection, you grow the confidence to play alone and explore the world—even if you're just across the room from your caregiver. You experience the excitement of discovering your own agency by moving your body and moving your toys.

But in an instant, that excitement can turn to fear.

A truck roars by the house. A startling noise crashes from another room. That furry thing—your cat—scratches you. Fear, panic, or loneliness suddenly consume you, even though you don't have those words yet.

All the joy evaporates. All the positive energy in your nervous system stops. It's all replaced by bad feelings. You have switched into protection mode, and your senses are at high alert, your breathing quickens, and your heart is beating faster. You are ready to fight or flee.

You now have an urgent need to connect with someone who can help you return to joy. You need help because you don't know how to calm down on your own.

If the distress is small, just checking in with eye contact from across the room is enough to calm your startled nervous system. If the distress is bigger, a soothing voice or reconnection through physical touch might help.

Whatever the distress, the attuned caregiver will help you return to joy. And these accumulated experiences of returning to joy—whether big or little—all grow your capacity for joyful connection.[9]

This is how you can learn to experience more joy and increase your capacity for joyful connection. The more experiences you have of returning to joy, the more capacity you have for experiencing not-joy moments and still returning to joy. These experiences of joyful connection shape your brain and body, building the capacity and elasticity of your sympathetic and parasympathetic nervous systems so they become flexible and adaptive rather than rigid or chaotic. These experiences of joyful connection help you efficiently move between connection and protection rather than getting stuck in protection mode.

God's Joyful Connection

Early in Israel's life, when Israel was just a baby nation, God gave instructions for how the high priest would regularly bless the people:

> The Lord bless you
>   and keep you;
> the Lord make his face shine on you
>   and be gracious to you;
> the Lord turn his face toward you
>   and give you peace.
>
> NUMBERS 6:24-26

God's face is mentioned twice in this blessing. That's a big deal, especially because in other places in the Old Testament we are told that no one can see God and live (see, for example, Exodus 33:20). In this blessing, we see that God's face is connected to both aspects of joyful connection—amplifying joy and returning to joy.

The Joy-Amplifying Face of God

First, this blessing offers us the joy-amplifying face of God. The blessing asks that "the Lord make his face shine on you and be gracious to you."

The idea of a face that shines on us is really something like the "beaming face," the "face with eyes dancing," or the "joyful face." This verse speaks of a joyful, face-to-face interaction with God. It's like that joy-amplifying reunion of Soren and Tennyson after day camp and our shining faces delighting in their joy.

Interestingly, this isn't the only place where the Bible speaks this way. Psalm 21:6 speaks of how God has granted the king of Israel "unending blessings and made him glad with the joy of your [God's] face." And Psalm 16:11 says of God, "You make known to me the path of life; before your face there is fullness of joy" (ESV).

Now, if you were to look up these verses, you might see the word *presence* instead of *face*. Why?

It's because Bible translators are trying to hold two things in tension. On the one hand, these verses (and others like them) use the Hebrew word for face (*pānîm*) when speaking of God. But on the other hand, these translators want us to remember what God told Moses: "You cannot see my face, for no one may see me and live" (Exodus 33:20, 23). Because of this, some Bible translators substitute *presence* when they come across the word for *face*.

This is why it is so striking that God gives us a blessing in which, not once but *twice*, we are told that God's face is looking upon us. The first time is God's joy-amplifying face that beams down on us.

The Returning-to-Joy Face of God

Second, this blessing assures us of the returning-to-joy face of God. The blessing asks that "the LORD turn his face toward you and give you peace."

When you are distressed, overwhelmed, full of fear, or feeling abandoned, God's face will turn toward you, comfort you, and give you peace. God's gaze soothes our distress when, like the little boy at church, we stumble or run into trouble.

This peace God gives is not just the absence of distress. It is the fullness of life. It is the peace we experience when life with others, with God, and with the world is flourishing. This is the peace that Jesus came to offer us—a peace that leads us into the very presence of God. It is the peace that "will guard your hearts and your minds in Christ Jesus" (Philippians 4:7).

So, if we are designed to desire joyful connection, ultimately it is God who wants to fulfill this desire in us. God's face shines upon us to amplify our joy and to help us return to joy. No matter what our experience of early life is like, joy is always available in the face of God turned toward us.

Reflection

COGNITIVE

What new ideas and thoughts stand out to you about faces and infant attachment?

How have you observed this in families you know?

What makes better sense to you after reading this? What do you find confusing?

Where do you feel challenged or in conflict with an idea?

AFFECTIVE

What are you feeling after reading about what's intended to happen between parents and infants? (Search online for "feelings wheel" to help you with words.)

As you reflect on what you know about your own childhood, what emotions come up for you?

How did your body respond to what you read?

Did you feel yourself slipping into protection mode? If so, what were you reading when you did?

Did anything you read bring you calm and connection? What was it? (Note: If you're a parent and you're noticing any sense of remorse over the way you parented in infancy and early childhood, keep reading. Encouragement is coming!)

FAITH

How does the idea of God's face turned toward you connect with your experience of God and of following Jesus?

What sounded like good news to you?

If you were to have a conversation with Jesus (or another member of the Trinity) about this chapter, what would you want to talk about?

CHAPTER 3

TWO DIMENSIONS: INTIMACY & INDEPENDENCE

Geoff dove into the pool, along with eight other boys in elementary school. He raced to the other side—the long way—of the Olympic-sized pool. Having spent all summer at the public pool, Geoff knew he was fast, certainly faster than the boys he was racing. When he touched the edge and came up for air, Geoff expected to be way ahead of the others. But he wasn't. In fact, he had finished second. All his confidence evaporated in confusion and anger.

As Geoff was getting out of the pool, a lifeguard walked over and whispered, "You would have won if you had used your legs." In all the excitement about the race, and with the expectation of winning, Geoff had forgotten how to swim—all arms, no legs.

Too often, in our relationships with others and with God, we are all arms and no legs. Or all legs and no arms. In part 2, we will explain how our attachments can go wrong and why some of us tend to use only one or the other. But right now, let's focus on how God meant for us to use both together.

As we swim around in our relationships, instead of using arms and legs, we use *intimacy* and *independence.*

Intimacy and Independence

In the last chapter, we focused on our desire for joyful connection. Joyful connection—cultivated through amplifying joy and returning to joy—is the foundation of secure attachment.

Two different but related dimensions of secure attachment are *intimacy* and *independence*. While these words might be familiar to you, let's take a minute to clarify what we mean when we use them.[1]

When we say *intimacy*, we don't mean sexual intimacy. Instead, intimacy is a sense of emotional closeness and trust. When you are intimate with someone, you can be vulnerable and honest, knowing you are loved and safe in their presence. You can have intimacy that goes both ways with a good friend, a sibling, or a spouse. You can offer intimacy to someone else when you hold space for them to be vulnerable and open and create an atmosphere of safety and acceptance. You can also find intimacy in a mentor or a counselor who creates this space for you.

When we say *independence*, we don't mean doing whatever you want, anytime you want. That is isolation and autonomy. Instead, independence is a sense of being distinct from other people, capable of acting on your own behalf and on behalf of others. You are a separate individual from the people around you, offering your unique thoughts and gifts and asking for what you need and want. You know you are unique, and you are comfortable in being different from the people around you while also being connected to people in relationships.[2]

We want to encourage you to think of both of these words as neutral. They are neither positive nor negative. They simply describe something that can become a positive or negative aspect of your life, depending on whether they are integrated or unbalanced.

God designed us to be deeply intimate (close, vulnerable, and trusting with one another) while still remaining independent (unique and distinguishable from one another). Like swimming with both our arms and legs, we navigate relationships as God created us to when we use both intimacy and independence. When these two dimensions are integrated and effective, we flourish in our relationships with others and with God. When intimacy and independence disintegrate or fight against each other, we flounder.

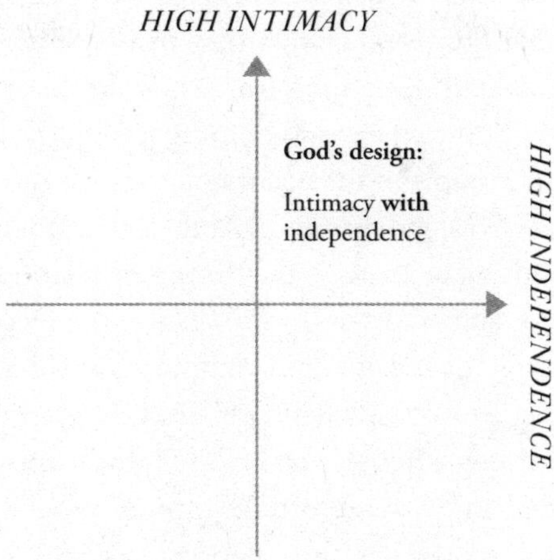

Growing Intimacy and Independence

Let's return to the experience of a baby and parent holding eye contact, seeing how joyful connection helps develop the dimensions of intimacy and independence.

You, as a baby, initiated connection by waving your arms and smiling in order to get the attention of your parents. The goal was to amplify joy by locking eyes and sharing smiles. That is pursuing *intimacy*—a felt sense of connection, belonging, and acceptance.

But when your nervous system became overstimulated by too much eye contact, you looked away. This is a small practice of *independence*. You were taking care of yourself.

Or when you were playing alone as a toddler, you were practicing your *independence* as you moved around and played with toys. You were discovering life as distinct from your parents, exercising independence as you saw fit. But when you became distressed by a loud noise, fell over, or just felt more alone than you wanted, you would seek *intimacy*—even if that was just eye contact across the room or hearing a voice from the doorway.

As a child, you didn't seek intimacy only when you needed help returning to joy. Often you would seek intimacy to amplify the joy that came through your independent action. This is why children constantly show parents what they found, what they made, or what they learned to do. They are taking something from their world of independence and bringing it back into the world of intimacy. It's the intimacy of the attachment relationship and the history of joyful connection that gives them the courage to be independent. And it's their independence that gives them something to share in their intimate relationship.

In adolescence and adulthood, you practiced independence by getting a driver's license or taking public transportation, hanging out with friends, or finding a job. But whether it was with your parents or with some other attachment figure, you also sought intimacy to help you navigate problems, understand relationships, or process pain. In every phase of life, you've moved in intimacy and independence, depending on your environment and where you received support and encouragement.[3]

God's Image in Us

Amazingly, this exactly aligns with what the Bible says about humanity being made in the image of God (the *imago Dei*). Sometimes people speak as though the image of God has to do with our immaterial souls, our rational minds, or our creative spirits. More recently, people point to our relational and communal capacities. In a sense, all of these are correct.

But more specifically, when Genesis speaks of the creation of humanity, two dominant themes arise: presence and purpose.[4] We are made for God's presence, and we are meant to extend God's purposes in the world. The first theme, that we are made to be with God, is seen when God places humanity in the Garden (see Genesis 2:8-15). God is present, walking with humanity in the cool of the day (see Genesis 3:8). The idea is that we were meant to be priests who belong in God's presence. The second theme, that we are made to extend God's loving purposes to the entire world, is seen in God giving humanity the authority to rule over the earth (see Genesis 1:28). People were meant to be royal representatives of God's Kingdom. Being made in God's image means being priests in God's presence and royal representatives of God's purposes. Or, in the language of attachment, we were made for intimacy with God and for independence alongside God.

You might feel like your capacity for closeness with God is pretty small. Maybe you haven't believed it's possible. Maybe you've been so shaped by your early years that you don't expect intimacy or even know how to spot it when you see it. But you are designed to be intimately connected to God and others. Becoming deeply attached to God will develop this dimension of your life.

God also designed you for independence. God doesn't want puppets or slaves or minions to boss around. This is why God gave humans the capacity for independence. You might feel like your capacity for independence is small. You might even resist the idea that you should practice independence in your relationship with God. *Aren't we supposed to depend on God?* you might ask. To answer that, we could say we are made for independence *alongside* God, but never independence *against* God. God made humanity as partners, not puppets.

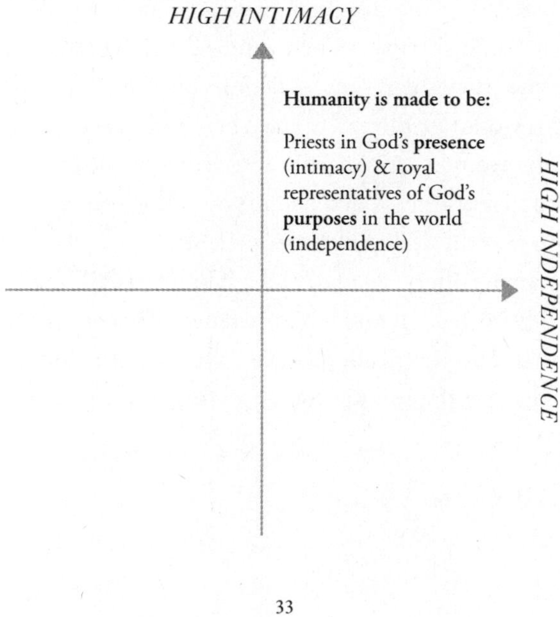

Care and Courage: What Attachment Figures Do

To better understand this connection between intimacy and independence, let's look at it from the parent's side.[5]

Parents offer intimacy and independence to their children in the form of *care* and *courage*.

Nadia has four kids, aged seven and under. She spends a lot of time offering *care* to them. She greets them with hugs and kisses in the morning, rubs their backs throughout the day, cuddles with them while reading books, and helps them find language for their emotions when they are trying to express something. This care is how intimacy begins to feel familiar and *safe*, growing into a sense of belonging. When parents offer this care, attachment research says they are acting like a *safe haven*.

Parents also offer *courage* for independence. Nadia has worked hard to make her house a structured environment for her kids to practice independence. She has pictures of food options the kids can pick for their meals, photos above toy bins so they can find things on their own, hooks with their initials above them so they can be responsible for their coats. When her daughter, Sadie, was nervous about going to a neighbor's birthday party, she encouraged her by telling Sadie how brave she is and how she is such a friendly and welcoming person that her neighbor would be blessed to have her at her party. She reminded Sadie that she would be right next door if she needed to come home for a minute to recharge. When parents offer this courage, attachment research says they are acting like a *secure base*.

When parents offer care in distress, it leads to children feeling safe (which builds intimacy), and when parents offer courage for discovery, it leads to children feeling brave (which builds independence). This is all built on the foundation of joyful connection.

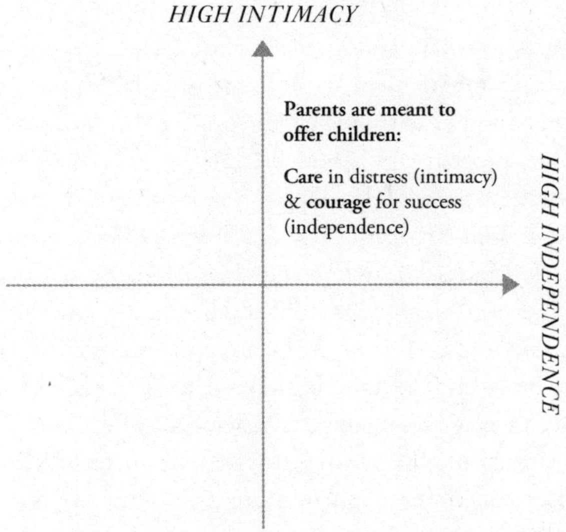

Over time, these two dimensions are meant to work together. As you were growing up, you needed to do more apart from your parents. You learned to use the bathroom, dress yourself, and pick up after yourself. At first, your parents helped you with these things. You did them together. But over time, your parents became less involved, and you did them on your own. Your world expanded as you went to day camps or friends' houses or school. You became more distinct from your parents as you operated independently. But you carried that intimate connection with you throughout your day, knowing that the relationship was strong and ready to receive you when you returned.

God, as a loving attachment figure, acts just this way toward us.

Children develop the dimensions of . . .	Intimacy	Independence
When parents offer them . . .	Care ("I'm here.")	Courage ("You can do it.")
Because as God's image bearers, we live . . .	In God's presence ("I am with you always"; see Matthew 28:20.)	For God's purposes ("Your Kingdom come"; see Matthew 6:10.)

God Is Our Attachment Figure

God promises Abraham and Sarah they will have a son. But Abraham and Sarah become impatient about God's promise, so they use Hagar as a surrogate mother to jumpstart the process (see Genesis 16:1-16). After getting pregnant by Abraham, Hagar runs away because of Sarah's bitterness and cruelty. Hagar flees to the wilderness, hoping for nothing more than death. And that is where God meets her.

God sees, hears, and understands Hagar's distress. God *cares* for her with kind words about her child and her future. These words give Hagar the *courage* to return to Abraham and Sarah. Throughout this interaction between God and Hagar, God acts as a loving attachment figure, offering care and courage to a beloved child.

Much later in the history of God's people, we meet Moses. As an adult, Moses encounters God in a burning bush. He is wandering and unwanted because he fled Egypt after murdering a man who was persecuting a fellow Hebrew. But God doesn't abandon or reject Moses. Rather, God comes to Moses as a loving attachment figure—and an attachment figure not just for Moses but for all the enslaved Hebrews in Egypt.

God tells Moses, "I have surely seen the affliction of my people . . . and have heard their cry. . . . I know their sufferings" (Exodus 3:7, ESV). God sees, hears, and understands what the Hebrews are going through. This is clear language of attunement, showing that God is attached to his people. God isn't distant and aloof. God is deeply concerned—like a parent—with the welfare of Israel, his firstborn son (see Exodus 4:22). Not only attuned and attentive, God is going to act: "I have come down to rescue them from the power of the Egyptians and lead them out of Egypt into their own fertile and spacious land. It is a land flowing with milk and honey" (Exodus 3:8, NLT). As an act of intimacy toward Israel, God comes near to offer comfort and care. And as an act of independence on behalf of Israel, God comes down to rescue them from Egypt.

The entire Old Testament is a witness to God as our attachment figure, where God is both our comfort in distress and our confidence to go out in faith and obedience. When we are deeply attached to God, we receive care and courage, which builds our capacity for intimacy and independence.

But growing in these dimensions takes work and is a process. So we need to dig a little deeper into what is happening in our brains and our bodies as we grow.

Window of Tolerance

In the last chapter, we talked about how your capacity for joy and your tolerance for distress expands through experiences of amplifying joy and returning to joy. As your capacity and tolerance expand, you are able to tolerate bigger and more complex emotions, and you learn to navigate the ups and downs of life.

How well you can handle big and complex emotions is called your *window of tolerance*.[6] When you have consistently experienced joyful connection, your window is wide and you are able to better handle the highs and lows of life without becoming emotionally distressed. When you have experienced less joy, your window is narrow, and you are more easily overwhelmed and distressed.

Think of water. In liquid form, it can flow and adapt to its environment. Its window of tolerance is between freezing and boiling—the points at which liquid water turns into ice or steam. When water turns to ice, it no longer flows. It is sluggish and stuck. But when water boils, it erupts everywhere.

Inside your window of tolerance, you can tolerate life because you have the capacity for it. You are floating down the river of life, flexibly navigating and adjusting to the situation. Inside the window of tolerance, the higher and lower parts of your brain and body can function together. Your cognitive thoughts and your affective experiences are integrated. Floating on the water, you feel like you. You act and respond in ways that keep you both intimate and independent. You can flexibly and appropriately shift between connection and protection.

WINDOW OF TOLERANCE

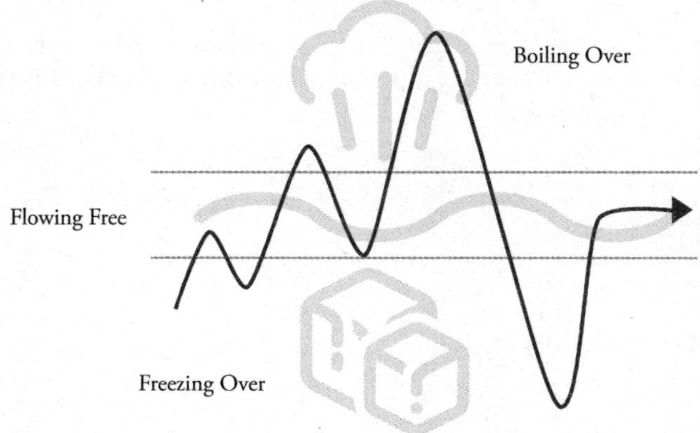

Outside your window of tolerance, you shift mostly into protection. This happens when something is happening around you, within you, or between you and another person that feels too big for you to handle. In response, your sympathetic nervous system kicks in, and you might feel hyperactivated—full of energy that makes you want to fight or flee. This is the water boiling over, erupting. You are exploding out the top of your window of tolerance. This is what happened when Cyd was waiting for Geoff and started pacing. She felt loads of energy coursing through her body. But sometimes your parasympathetic nervous system takes over and you might check out, shut down, disconnect, or disassociate. This is the water freezing over. You feel like you've run out of the energy to handle your life. This is the feeling of falling out the bottom of your window of tolerance. This happened when Geoff still hadn't arrived and Cyd began to collapse.

In general, when you are outside your window of tolerance, you don't feel like you. You act and react in ways you don't understand and maybe later regret. When you are outside your window of tolerance, you are no longer resourceful. You are in survival mode. When this happens, it is called dysregulation. Breaking through the top or bottom edge of your window of tolerance can also be thought of as erupting into chaos (boiling over the top) or getting stuck in rigidity (becoming ice at the bottom).[7]

Rupture and Repair

What does all this window of tolerance stuff have to do with intimacy and independence?

Every time you break through the top or bottom edge of your window of tolerance, you experience a rupture. A rupture can be anything from physical distress (like being hungry, tired, or overstimulated) to a relational disruption (like having a little misunderstanding or a major betrayal). Any of these are ruptures.

You might think the goal of life is never to experience ruptures, especially with other people. But this is impossible. In fact, about 70 percent of the time we are out of sync with the people around us, causing small or large ruptures.[8] If you try to avoid all ruptures all the time, you will exhaust yourself, come off as controlling, and actually stunt the development of your relationships. The desire to avoid all ruptures is what drives you into unhealthy attachment landscapes.

It is *repair* that is the defining moment. In fact, it is repairing ruptures that grows your window of tolerance, allowing you to handle larger and more complex emotions and situations. The repair process is what helps you grow and mature. When a relationship has a history of ruptures being repaired, you grow in your capacity to endure discomfort and distress because you know that the rupture can be repaired. You trust the history of rupture and repair. And that gives you hope for the future.

WIDE WINDOW

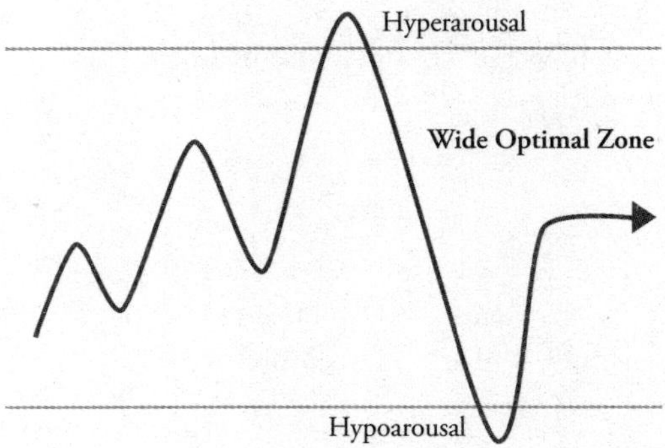

For example, as a kid, you master the independence of staying in bed when you wake up at night. But during a big storm, you might rush to your parents' room because you are distressed. This is using intimacy to repair a rupture that occurred during independence. This repair both strengthens your intimacy with your parents (provided they offer comfort) and increases your confidence to stay in bed next time, knowing that Mom and Dad are available if you need them.

As an adult, when you feel too vulnerable or overwhelmed while pursuing intimacy, you may need to pull back for a moment and slow the conversation down. This is a rupture that is repaired by drawing from your capacity for independence. This rupture strengthens your ability to engage in intimacy once again after you've taken a moment to recalibrate.

Integrated Intimacy and Independence

Just as Geoff couldn't swim effectively while using only his arms, you can't live into God's good design with an overreliance on either intimacy or independence. Picture a grid that is made up of two dimensions: intimacy and independence. The vertical line represents intimacy. The closer you are to the top, the larger your capacity for intimacy. The horizontal line represents independence. The closer you are to the right side, the more confident you are to act independently.

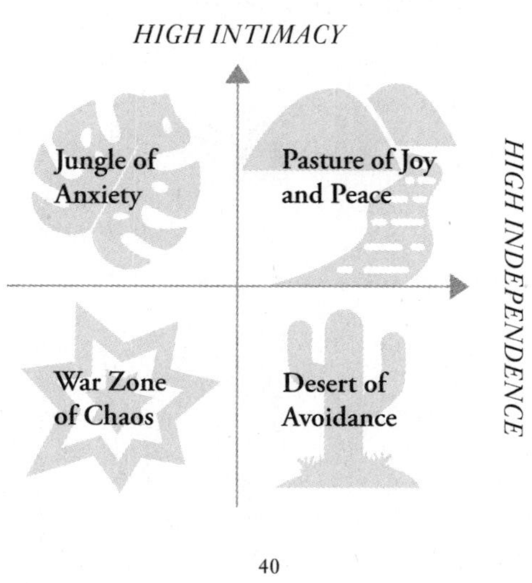

While the two dimensions are distinct from each other, they are related. The more you develop in secure attachment, the more you will find yourself in the top right quadrant, comfortable with intimacy and confident in your independence. This is the Pasture of Joy and Peace.

But sometimes—because of childhood environments that lead to insecure attachment—you develop strategies that prioritize one at the expense of the other. If you prioritize pursuing intimacy but struggle with independence, this is living in what we will call the Jungle of Anxiety (top left). But if you exercise a lot of independent action but struggle to be intimate, this is living in what we will call the Desert of Avoidance (bottom right). If you have struggled to create any kind of consistent strategies, you might find yourself in the War Zone of Chaos (bottom left). We will get into these attachment landscapes more specifically in part 2.

But before we do, it's important to pause here and remember what we are doing in this section of the book. We're laying out God's good design for your relational attachments. God made you to be joyfully connected with God and with people, comfortable with intimacy and confidently independent. When this is the case, you can effectively love God, others, and even yourself. These are the benefits of being securely attached.

As you read this, you might already be starting to identify ways that you are missing joyful connection, are uncomfortable with intimacy, or lack confidence in independence. It's okay. Breathe. You're not too far gone. You're not a lost cause. Remember, you developed the strategies you're labeling "wrong" or "broken" because they worked for you. They helped you survive. In this light, they were the "right" strategies for you when you needed them. Everyone has them. You're not alone. And God is inviting you—yes, *you*—into the Pasture of Joy and Peace. Stay with us. We're moving toward the Pasture together.

Reflection

COGNITIVE

How are these explanations of intimacy and independence different from how you have understood them? What do you find helpful about these explanations? What do you find confusing?

What feels like confirmation of your own experience?

Where do you feel challenged or in conflict with an idea?

AFFECTIVE

What are you feeling after reading about how you're designed to grow strong in both intimacy and independence? (Search online for "feelings wheel" to help you identify your feelings.)

How did your body respond to what you read? Did you feel yourself slipping into protection mode? If so, what were you reading when you did?

Did anything you read bring you calm and connection? What was it?

FAITH

How does learning about God's desire to be intimate with you connect with your experience of God and of following Jesus? What about God's desire to give you independence?

What sounded like good news to you?

If you were to have a conversation with Jesus (or another member of the Trinity) about this chapter, what would you want to talk about?

CHAPTER 4

THREE DEFAULTS: FAITH, HOPE, LOVE

I hit my head hard, rolled, and landed on my back. I (Geoff) had broken my collarbone and bruised my ego. What happened?

What kept me safe on a mountain bike caused an accident on a motorcycle.

Before becoming an inexperienced motorcyclist, I was a fairly experienced bicyclist. On a mountain bike, the back-wheel brake is operated by squeezing a lever on the right handlebar. I could fly down a mountain and perfectly control my speed by opening and closing the back-wheel brake with my right hand. I would do it without thinking because riding a bike was part of my implicit-procedural memory—like tying my shoes. I had a well-developed working model in my brain and body of how to ride a bike.

But on a motorcycle, the right hand does not control the back-wheel brake. It controls the front-wheel brake.

I was on a gravel road, going downhill, and I needed to slow down to keep from running into a vehicle in front of me. I was already mashing down the back-wheel brake on the right-foot pedal. Hard. But I needed more braking.

At this point, my brain was moving fast—*very* fast. My internal crisis level had shifted from mild concern to near panic. Connection mode was out the window. It was all protection now. And protection works through the much faster implicit memory (the acting-without-thinking memory).

In an instant, I switched back to my how-to-ride-a-mountain-bike model of the world. I squeezed with my right hand, expecting back-wheel braking. But instead, it activated the front-wheel brake—the one thing I didn't want to do going downhill on gravel.

So I flew off the motorcycle because my conscious and explicit how-to-drive-a-motorcycle mind shifted back to my subconscious and implicit how-to-ride-a-mountain-bike memory. I crashed because my old mental model of mountain biking spontaneously activated an old behavior that was useful in the past (it produced safety) but catastrophic in the present (it caused an injury). There was nothing wrong with my old mental model. It protected me in the past. But when I used it in a context where it didn't fit, it caused me harm.

We all have mental models like this. They are shaped by our life experiences and serve as our defaults. And when we move into our acting-without-thinking memory, we live from these defaults.

We've All Got Defaults

These defaults are collections of explicit (conscious) and implicit (subconscious) memories and processes. Defaults are semiautomatic habits, skills, expectations, and reactions that make life efficient and predictable. They help us navigate relationships, manage expectations, and solve problems. These defaults become the stories we live from, shaping and coloring our experiences and giving meaning and significance to our lives. And sometimes one default might be in conflict with another default, just like Geoff's older default for riding a bike conflicted with his newer default for riding a motorcycle.

Generally, we *feel* these defaults in our bodies, in our emotions. We just *know* how to react (implicit processing) even before we can *say* what is happening (explicit processing). These feelings and reactions are embedded in our brains and bodies. They don't feel like choices. They have become the default setting. These defaults could be connected to riding a bike, cooking a meal, or greeting a loved one. Or they could relate to driving a car.

Depending on where you live in the world, you drive on one side of the road or the other. In the United States, the default is the right side. But in England, it's the left side. A related default in the United States is to look left first when crossing a street because that's where the cars are coming from. But in England, you would look to the right first. So depending on which side of the road cars drive on, pedestrians learn different habits for crossing the street. One set of defaults (about where to drive a car) is connected to another set of defaults (about how to cross a street).

Our attachment defaults are connected in a similar way.

Designed Attachment Defaults (Little Experiments)

People are all little scientists. Throughout your life, you run little experiments to figure out how relationships work. The data you collect helps you figure out what to expect from the world and from others, and what you contribute to it all. As a little kid—even as an infant—you were a keen observer and a clever scientist.

When Tennyson was about a year old, we would put him in his high chair with a few toys while lunch was being made. Tennyson, as a little scientist, would run experiments about intimacy and independence with his brother. He would knock a toy off the tray. Then Soren, who was two and a half, would say, "Uh oh," pick it up, and put it back on Tennyson's tray. Tennyson smiled and giggled. He did it again. And Soren returned the dropped toy. Now Tennyson knocked *two* toys off the tray. Soren picked up both of them. Tennyson squealed with delight! Through playing with his brother, Tennyson was learning how his independent actions connected to intimacy with his brother. When lunch was ready, other experiments would start, this time about what foods to eat, how to eat them, and what would happen if food was dropped on the floor like the toys.

Your early joyful connections, your experiences of intimacy and independence, and these cycles of rupture and repair are all data points that slowly form your sense of how other people work, how the world works, and how you work. In his quest to discover what amplifies joy and what decreases distress, Tennyson was gathering data. You did the same thing.

You create attachment defaults—or really, they are created in you—as you adapt to your early relational environments and experiences. These attachment defaults act as filters for your thoughts and emotions. They highlight some things, ignore others, and sometimes get rid of information that doesn't seem useful. These defaults color what you perceive, experience, feel, think, and remember about your relationships with *others*, the *world*, and *yourself*.[1]

DEVELOPMENT—GOD'S DESIGN

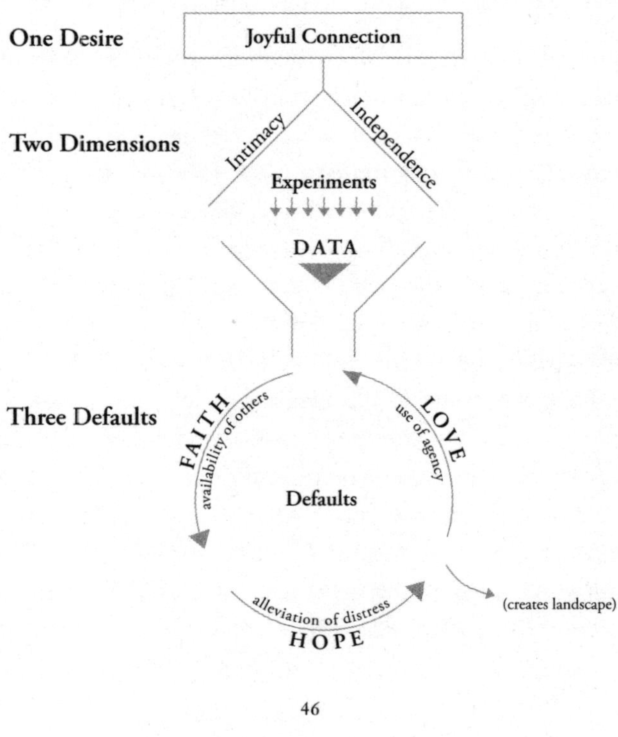

Attachment research has identified three core attachment defaults, often called *internal working models*.[2] We can state them in the form of three questions:

- *Are others available when I'm in distress?*
- *Will this distress be alleviated?*
- *How do I use my agency amid the distress?*

Just like the best way to cross a street is connected to which side of the road you drive on, these three attachment defaults all work together. Let's go through them one at a time.

Default #1: Are Others Available?

The first attachment default is focused on *other people*.

As a little scientist, every interaction with your attachment figures gives you a new piece of data. When you have attuned and attentive caregivers, regularly experience joyful connection, and have your ruptures regularly repaired as you return to joy, you get a lot of data saying that others will be available when you are in distress—no matter what. This becomes part of your reality. Your default is to *know* that others are there for you.

Over time, this implicit default that others are available grows into a general sense of belonging. You live from the embodied sense that *I fit here; I belong here*, that you are accepted and acceptable. You have a felt sense that others are with you and for you. When it comes to the implicit question of *Will others be available to me?* you have the answer *yes* stored deep in your body and your brain.

This yes is like a green light on the road of relationships, on the road of life. Green means go. Green means it is safe to proceed. Green means life is moving forward. Of course, you need to pay attention while driving. And sometimes you need to hit the brakes. But your *default* green light toward relationships means you keep moving, keep exploring, keep opening up, and keep being optimistic.

This yes literally shapes your nervous system and defines the way you see the world. Based on this yes, you feel supported and encouraged, even when you're not with your people. This feeling that others are available to you is part of what it means to feel safe. You carry this sense of belonging and others' availability in the confidence you take with you everywhere you go.

We all have a fundamental need to belong. This need is what drives us to seek community and follow cultural norms, and it is why we bend to peer pressure. But our need to belong is less about fitting in and more about finding the people who are available to us. We need to *see* and *feel* that we belong when we need help, when we are overwhelmed, or when we are stressed out. People need to *demonstrate*, through actions, that we matter to them.

Building a sense of belonging through being told you are accepted might make you feel good in the short run. And it is relatively easy for people to say. But this pales in comparison to *being shown* you belong when people are available to you when you are in distress and need help. Over time, when people are truly available and present to you in real ways, you learn that you belong. You gain confidence in your faith in the availability of your people.

God's good design is that you would *know* and *believe* at the default level—implicitly in your body and brain—that *others are available*. This is the first internal working model, the first designed default.

Default #2: Will This Stress Be Alleviated?

The second designed default is focused on your expectations about the *world*. When you are in distress, you cry out for help. You throw out signals into the world. You communicate your discomfort or displeasure in some way. Then you wait. And you hope.

In sending out distress signals, you are not only running experiments to find out if others are available. You are also gathering information about the question, *Will the distress ever end? Will I always feel this way?* In other words, is the world full of pain and danger that lasts? Or is discomfort only temporary?

In a secure attachment relationship, someone will help you return to joy. Maybe not as fast as you want or in the way you wanted, but someone alleviates distress by helping you find a solution you can live with. The world becomes livable again. This is the process of repairing ruptures, of returning to joy. Regular experiences of moving from distress back to joy create the implicit expectation that distress will be alleviated. The world is not always dangerous and full of lasting pain. Your nervous system is being trained and stretched to anticipate the relief of distress. You learn that discomfort and distress are temporary. They won't last forever. You can make it through.[3]

As you read this, you might be thinking, *But distress* isn't *always alleviated!* This is true. Chronic pain is real, ruptures between family members persist, poverty and food scarcity don't always go away. But when a person sees your distress and is in it with you, you realize you're not alone. Your distress is seen, known, and understood, and somebody is doing something about it—whether comforting you or taking action to remove the distress. Your relationships are stronger than anything the world can throw at you. Knowing that distress won't last forever gives you courage to persevere in the suffering.

God's good design is for you to believe—implicitly in your body and brain—that distress will be alleviated. This is the second internal working model, the second designed default.

Default #3: How Do I Use My Agency?

The third designed default is focused on your *agency*, on your sense of being able to act in the world. When you are a baby in distress, you cry out for help. You are the one who acts. You are putting something into the world to see what happens. You are the scientist, running experiments and collecting data. And when someone responds to you, you are the one who made that happen. Through a secure attachment relationship, you start developing a sense of your *agency* and how it connects to *others* and the *world*.

Sometimes you use your agency to pursue intimacy. Sometimes you use it to practice independence.

As you get older and can move and talk, you can act to solve your own problems sometimes. You can move closer to your parents when you are frightened. You can find your own food when you are hungry. You can decide to share your toys with a sibling. You have agency that can change the world.

Sometimes, when you are in distress, you act to get help from others. You can't solve the problem by yourself, so you use your agency to find someone bigger, stronger, and safer to help you. Someone who can make the food. Someone who can solve the "he's not sharing" problem with your sibling. You have agency that helps you connect with others.

God's good design is for you to *know*—implicitly in your body and brain—that you have agency to integrate intimacy and independence for your own good and for the good of others and the world. You have the power to explore and impact the world and stay connected to your people. This is the third internal working model, the third designed default.

Designed for Faith, Hope, and Love

These three defaults are God's good design for us. So it makes sense that they are all over the Bible. These attachment defaults align with faith, hope, and love. As Paul says, "Three things will last forever—faith, hope, and love—and the greatest of these is love" (1 Corinthians 13:13, NLT).

Faith

Faith is more than ideas. It's not just words we say or doctrines we agree with. To say, "I have faith in God" or "I believe in Jesus" is one thing. But living like God is available is different from saying, "I have faith."

In the Bible, faith is closer to trust, loyalty, or allegiance. Faith is a fully embodied commitment to someone. Faith is living as if this relationship is the most important thing. Faith is acting as if someone will be available when we are in distress. We have faith in someone when we spontaneously move toward them when we are distressed, confident of their availability.

This is why whenever Israel followed after other gods, the prophets called it adultery. Adultery is unfaithfulness to the relationship. The problem wasn't that Israel stopped believing that God existed. The problem was that Israel was trusting in other gods, trusting in idols. Israel broke faith with God. They didn't trust God.

We are designed to develop confident faith in God and faith in others. We see this kind of faith in God in Hebrews 11, which lists all the people who lived as if God was available to them. They trusted God's availability and God's promises so much that they built arks on dry land, left everything they knew to go where God sent them, hid babies in rivers, sprinkled lamb's blood on doorposts, set foot into the divided sea, marched around cities and waited for walls to fall, and were willing to endure torture and death because they refused to be unfaithful. "All these people earned a good reputation because of their faith, yet none of them received all that God had promised. For God had something better in mind for us" (Hebrews 11:39-40, NLT). We could say that all these heroes of faith were confidently persevering through suffering, trusting that God was attuned and available.

This absolute trust and loyalty is what allows us to "strip off every weight that slows us down, especially the sin that so easily trips us up," helping us to name our outdated survival strategies by "keeping our eyes on Jesus, the champion who initiates and perfects our faith" (Hebrews 12:1-2, NLT). It's this kind of faith that is God's good design for us.

Hope

Hope is more than wishing. "I hope it's sunny today" or "I hope it goes well" or "I hope I win the lottery" are expressions of things you would like to see happen.

But in the Bible, hope is an expectant waiting. It is expectant because it is full of faith in God (the first designed default). And it is waiting because it persists through time. Sometimes a lot longer than we want.

Hope and waiting are often used interchangeably in the Psalms. They are used as synonyms of each other. Here are two examples.

> I wait for the LORD, my whole being waits,
> and in his word I put my hope.
> I wait for the Lord
> more than watchmen wait for the morning,
> more than watchmen wait for the morning.
> Israel, put your hope in the LORD,
> for with the LORD is unfailing love
> and with him is full redemption.
>
> PSALM 130:5-7

Here hoping and waiting are connected, a waiting and hoping directed toward God. Specifically, hope is connected to the Lord's unfailing love (which alleviates distress) and is often called *redemption* (see the last word in verse 7).

> The eyes of the LORD are on those who fear him,
> on those whose hope is in his unfailing love,
> to deliver them from death
> and keep them alive in famine.
> We wait in hope for the LORD;
> he is our help and our shield.
> In him our hearts rejoice,
> for we trust in his holy name.
> May your unfailing love be with us, LORD,
> even as we put our hope in you.
>
> PSALM 33:18-22

Here we see that the Lord's eyes are looking on those who fear him. And those who fear God are really just those who hope in God's unfailing love, courageously expecting to be delivered from their distress. So hope means waiting on the Lord, believing that God will alleviate our distress. Because we have faith in God, we can wait expectantly for our present distress to be alleviated.

God designed us to develop unflinching, courageous hope, knowing that God—and others—will help alleviate our distress even as we wait for circumstances to change.

Love

Too often we treat love like a vague sentiment, a romantic infatuation, or a fervent feeling. Certainly, love includes feelings and emotions, usually a lot of them in complex layers.

But love, in the Bible and for attachment, focuses on action. We know someone loves us because they are available to us, giving us care in our distress and offering us courage for discovery.

This is why Paul, in the famous love chapter, uses verbs along with adjectives to describe love:

> Love is patient and kind. Love is not jealous or boastful or proud or rude. It does not demand its own way. It is not irritable, and it keeps no record of being wronged. It does not rejoice about injustice but rejoices whenever the truth wins out. Love never gives up, never loses faith, is always hopeful, and endures through every circumstance. . . . Love will last forever!
>
> 1 CORINTHIANS 13:4-8, NLT

Just as God's love for humanity is known through actions, we also share love through actions.

We are designed to overflow in love toward God and for others. When we are filled with the love of God, we can freely give it away to others through connecting. This is what our agency is for: loving

God and loving others. Our agency isn't only for pursuing our own interests. It's also for pursuing what is best for others. It isn't for circling the wagons of our self-protective survival strategies. It's also for ensuring the weak are protected. Our agency is designed for strong connections—love in action.

Designed Defaults in the Garden

We see Adam and Eve living from these designed defaults at the beginning of the Bible.

God walks and talks with Adam and Eve in the garden. God and humanity belong together. Adam and Eve belong together. They know they belong, and they have God and each other. Help is never far away. *Others are available. A confident faith is growing in them.*

God provides everything Adam and Eve need. They are safe and cared for. When they get hungry, there is food. When they are thirsty, there is water. No matter what discomfort they might experience, they know it is temporary. God will meet them every day, in their physical needs and in their need for companionship with him as they walk and talk in the cool of the day. *Distress will be alleviated. A courageous hope is growing in them.*

Adam and Eve have a purpose. God has given them authority and responsibility: to name animals, tend the garden, and make life flourish. They know that what they do matters. They have the power to affect the world around them, and they choose to use that power to do good for all of life in the garden. *They use their agency to bless the world. Love is flowing through them.*

This is how God designed us. We are supposed to know faith, hope, and love in our bones.

Because God First Attached to Us

Growing in faith, hope, and love is not something we can do by ourselves.

Without people who are available to us, who are able to alleviate our distress, and who empower us for agency, we cannot grow into these designed defaults. Because it is in relationships that our brains and bodies are shaped, these designed defaults are gifts placed within us by those who love us. These defaults of faith, hope, and love are nurtured in us through loving, attuned, and attentive experiences of intimacy and independence. They are created through receiving joyful connection.

This is why the Bible reminds us that we love God because God first loved us (see 1 John 4:19). God—with an everlasting, unfailing, and steadfast love—has given us everything we need so that we might develop the defaults of faith, hope, and love. In the language of attachment science, we become deeply attached to God because God is already deeply attached to us. Even if we didn't grow into God's designed defaults because we were missing things in our childhoods, God can repair our ruptures. God is available to us. God is going to alleviate our distress. And God empowers us to do the same for others. He loves first. God attaches to us and gives us what we need to grow in confident faith, courage, and connection!

Reflection

COGNITIVE

What do you think of this idea of defaults that shape the way you see the world, others, God, and yourself?

Based on what you see yourself doing in distress, what do you think your answers to these questions might be like?

What feels clearer to you about how you handle distress after reading this? What do you find confusing? What do you find yourself wanting to know more about?

AFFECTIVE

What are you feeling after reading about the defaults that God designed and how your answers to these questions might differ from the way you're designed to answer them? (Search online for "feelings wheel" to help put your finger on your emotions.)

What feels encouraging to consider? What feels threatening?

As you read, where did you notice yourself experiencing connection or protection?

FAITH

How does mapping the defaults to faith, hope, and love connect with your experience of God and of following Jesus? What sounded like good news to you?

If you were to have a conversation with Jesus (or another member of the Trinity) about this chapter, what would you want to talk about?

INTERLUDE

WHERE YOU ARE

At this point, let's summarize God's compelling vision for the way things are supposed to be. Then we'll talk about how things actually are.

We are designed, in our brains and our bodies, to be deeply attached to God and others. From the moment of our conception, our arrival is anticipated. As soon as we are born, we are received with gladness! As we seek out faces of joy, we find them everywhere. We have loving parents who smile at us, hold our gaze, and amplify our joy. Our parents' faces shine upon us, just as God's face does. Whenever we experience any kind of distress or discomfort, our parents turn their faces toward us and help us return to joy. Through the consistent joyful connection we experience with our parents, our windows of tolerance grow wide.

Because we have attuned parents, we grow in intimacy. We feel seen, heard, known, and loved. We know we are safe to be ourselves in our families because we are wanted and welcomed. We have a secure base to return to in times of distress. We are also brave enough to leave our safe harbor and explore our worlds independently. When we experience ruptures in our intimate relationships or in our independent explorations, those ruptures are repaired.

We *know*, deep in our bodies, that people are available to us. We have a sense of belonging to a community of people who are for us, even when we are not with them. Whenever we run into distress of any kind, it is consistently alleviated—either by the people in our lives or in our own capacity to care for ourselves. We are confident in our agency to act, not only for our own good but also for the good of the community we participate in.

Because of this solid foundation, our nervous system is wired to handle the world. We have what it takes. When we do find ourselves beyond the edges of our window of tolerance, we can choose whether we want to find people to help us regulate our emotions (*coregulation*) or whether we have the ability to calm ourselves (*solo regulation*). Because both options are available to us, we go through life self-regulated. We can experience a wide range of emotions without being overwhelmed. We can endure difficult circumstances without coming undone.

We are people of joy and peace. We know who we are. Others are drawn to us and enjoy spending time with us. We contribute to our communities in meaningful ways. Our faith runs deep. We *know* and find strength in the joy of God's gladness to be with us. We experience intimacy with God, sharing our deepest inner lives with Jesus, and we partner with God to bring life to everyone around us. We trust God's availability to us at all times, wait expectantly for God to alleviate distress, and use our agency to love the world like God does.

Dwelling in the Pasture of Joy and Peace, deeply attached to God. This is the life we were meant to live.

The Way Things Are: A World of Ruptures

But this is likely not your story.

It isn't our story either.

Ever since Adam and Eve, human beings have lived in ways that prioritize protection over connection. We all find ourselves in different places. Some of us are extremely happy with where we are. Some of us experience a lot of pain or confusion. Some of us are fairly numb.

The brokenness of the world runs deep. Bad things happen to us. We miss out on good things. Sometimes we can see and know and name the sin that surrounds us. Other times it's more subtle, or we don't have the language for it. Whatever the case, our survival strategies spring out of a world permeated with ruptures.

Your parents or caregivers developed their own survival skills based on their own lives, and they raised you in those environments. Unless they did a lot of work to sort through their own anxiety, avoidance, or chaos and developed a secure attachment with God and others, *their* insecure attachment strategies formed *your* insecure attachment strategies.

You didn't get where you are on your own. You got here by existing in relationships and learning strategies to survive—and sometimes thrive—in them.

God is not finished—with this world or with you. What we've described above is still God's dream for you. And even if you can't have a different past, you *can* have a different future. You can practice amplifying and returning to joy, you can grow in intimacy and independence, and your defaults can shift as you conduct new experiments with Jesus as your attachment figure.

But first, you need to find yourself where you are.

How to Read Part 2: Where You Find Yourself

In the coming chapters, we describe the four attachment landscapes: The Jungle of Anxiety, the Desert of Avoidance, the War Zone of Chaos, and the Pasture of Joy and Peace.

These landscapes are places you live in and live from. But these landscapes are not your identity or personality type. Unlike personality profiles that will name you with a four-letter combination, place you in a triad, or assign you a color, shape, or animal, these attachment landscapes are not defining.[1] Instead, they are descriptive of the way your history (or lack) of joyful connection and intimacy and independence have shaped your defaults to see and experience the world from a *yes*, *maybe*, or *no*. Your answer can change (see part 3).

DEVELOPMENT—GOD'S DESIGN

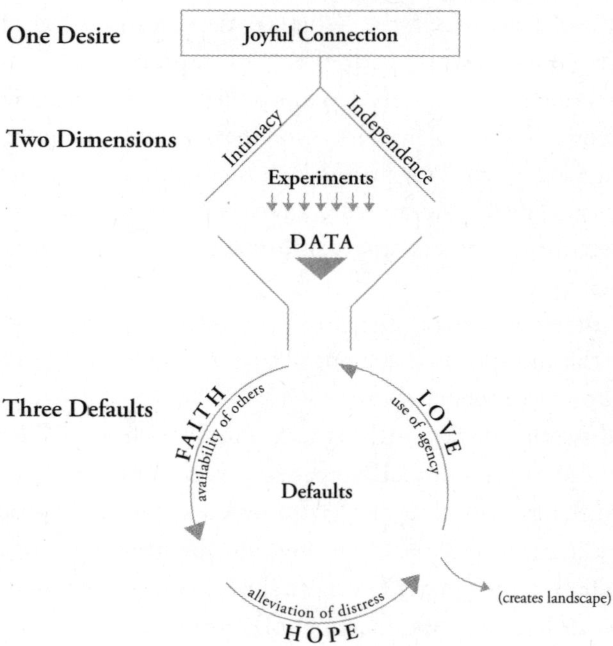

As you read the composite stories of people we've interacted with (names and details have been changed) and the descriptions of the landscapes, you may find that more than one landscape feels familiar to you. This might be because you had one parent who was in the Jungle and another who was from the Desert. Or you might have had a Desert parent *and* a Pasture grandparent who lived with you. Maybe you grew up in two different houses—one that was more of a Desert and one that was more of a War Zone. Kids are amazingly good at adapting to environments and doing what is needed to survive. It's entirely possible that you learned to switch landscapes because that's what your context demanded.

As you read these chapters, we hope you can find compassion for yourself and how you came to find yourself where you are. Notice which parts of each landscape resonate for you. Which stories describe your experience, both past and present? As much as possible, try not to evaluate or judge yourself. Instead, try to appreciate your ability to create the needed strategies to survive. Stay curious. Try to be open to how your strategies are both a gift and an obstacle to secure attachment with God.

Additionally, we hope you can find greater compassion for the people you live in relationship with and for the people in your local church community. Even if a landscape doesn't feel familiar to you, chances are high that you are in a relationship with someone in this landscape—whether in your home, your extended family, your local church, or your neighborhood. The more you can understand these four landscapes, the more understanding you can have of the survival skills others are employing that are no longer serving them.

If you've been reading this book on your own so far, we're glad you're here and want to celebrate your desire to deepen your attachment with God. There are practices here that you will need to do on your own. You're also going to need some people to do this with you. We want to encourage you to invite at least one other person to read with you. You will need to have some conversations with flesh-and-blood people.

If you've been reading this book with a group, we're glad you're here too! We want to celebrate your desire to deepen your attachment with God as well. We're glad you have people to do this with. You will also need to do some of this alone with God. As we move forward in the book, we'll offer some practices that will require you to be alone, to look inside, to bring what you find to God. We want to encourage you to do this *before* you bring your reflections to a group.

More than anything, we hope you find new inspiration to grow in your attachment with Jesus, your Good Shepherd. When you can identify the landscape you are living from, you can understand what new skills you need to learn in order to move into the Pasture of Joy and Peace. When you see how compelling the Pasture is, you will *want* to do the work to join Jesus in changing your defaults and growing more deeply attached to God.

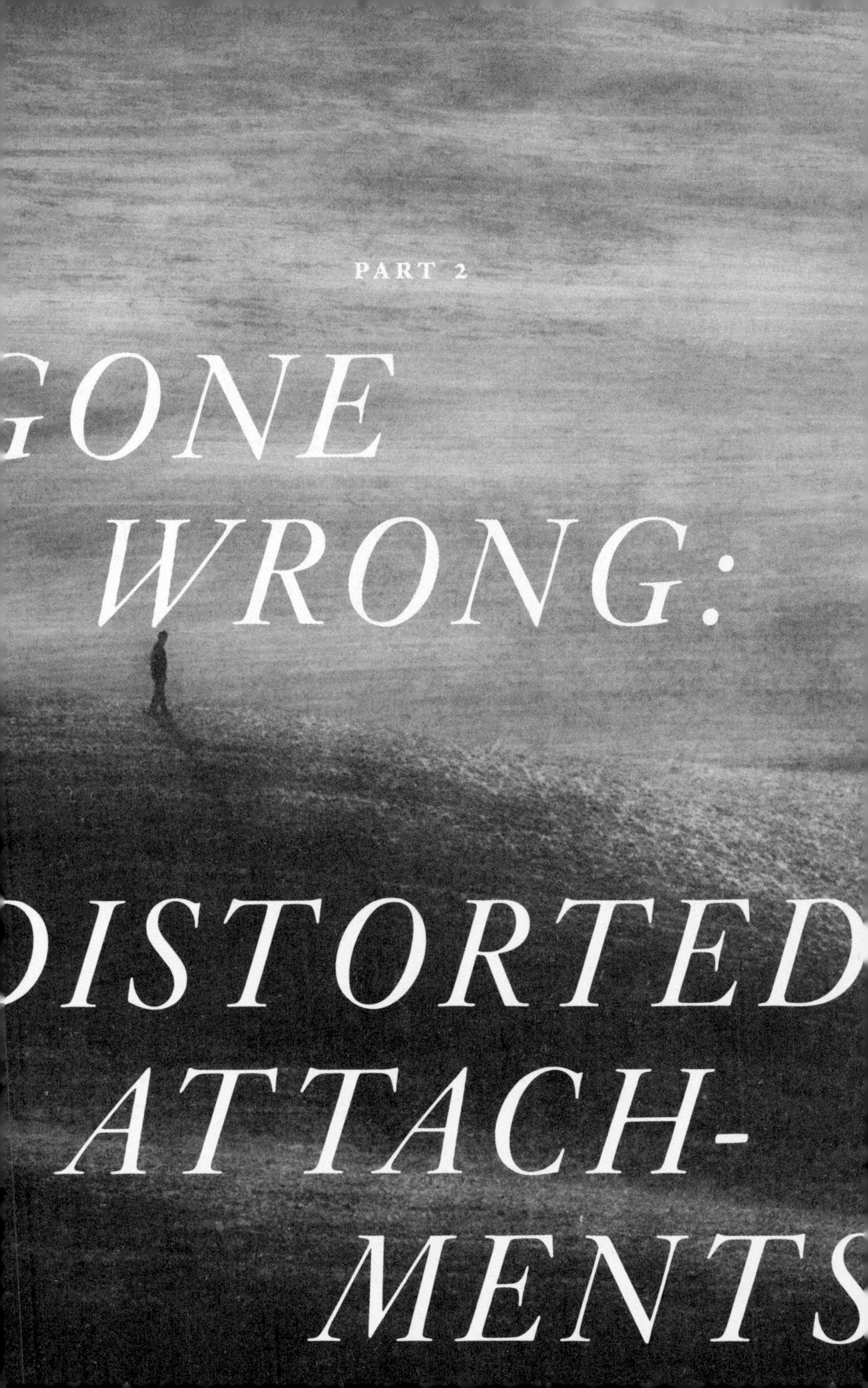

PART 2

GONE WRONG: DISTORTED ATTACHMENTS

CHAPTER 5

JUNGLE GOD: AN ANXIOUS FAITH

Abigail came to coaching with me (Cyd), saying, "I'm so tired of being where I am. I don't have my own foundation to stand on. Brandon [Abigail's husband] invited his teen daughter from a previous relationship to live with us a few months ago, and now he feels gone. I'm feeling abandoned, and I'm struggling with anxiety."

This capable and competent business owner was totally shaken by the perceived loss of intimacy when Brandon started splitting his attention between Abigail and Mia, his daughter from a previous relationship.

Abigail recognized that she was far more shaken up by this change than she should be. "I'm used to doing hard things. I should be able to roll with this. But I can't. When he spends time with Mia without me, I'm so anxious the whole time. I can't handle it. Something is wrong here."

Abigail's need for intimacy and connection with Brandon was being threatened by his relationship with his daughter. She could recognize this wasn't the way she wanted to live. She didn't want to be jealous and demanding. But she had no idea how to quiet the anxiety and celebrate Brandon's love for Mia.

As a child, Abigail had learned to survive in the Jungle of Anxiety. But as an adult, these survival skills were holding her back.

The Jungle

Imagine life in a jungle.

A jungle is filled with lush greenery, layers of trees and plants. There's water everywhere—moisture in the air, daily rain, abundant streams and waterfalls.

In the jungle, there are bright colors: Fruits hanging heavy from the trees, brightly colored flowers, brilliant bird feathers, dart frogs that look dipped in paint, moths as big as your head, and insects the size of your hand. The whole environment is a riot of color and texture. And the noise! If you've ever had a chance to visit a jungle, you know that day or night it's never quiet—buzzing insects, trilling frogs, calling birds, screeching monkeys, chirping crickets. It's constant.

The jungle is stunningly gorgeous. But it is also wild and unpredictable.

Maybe you grew up in a relational environment that was like a jungle. One moment your life was full of delights. The next moment things were difficult. One minute you were enjoying the beauty of everything around you. But then a torrential rain poured down and you ran for cover.

If you grew up in a jungle, your nervous system was shaped by it. Your history of joyful (or lack of joyful) connection and your early experiments with intimacy and independence shaped your attachment defaults. Growing up in a relational and emotional jungle has led you into an anxious faith with a Jungle god.

Growing Up in the Jungle of Anxiety

The attachment Jungle comes from inconsistent caregiving. Your parents were sporadically attuned to your attempts for joyful connection. And they were unpredictably attentive to your distress. Sometimes they amplified joy through connection and helped you return to joy in distress. But many times they didn't.

Growing up in the Jungle, you found that the people who loved you were intermittently present and available. Sometimes your parents were encouraging and excited for you. But sometimes they weren't. They played with you, took an interest in your interests, hugged you, and affirmed you—and it felt great. But then they were checked out—too busy, too tired, too sick. They had their own stuff going on, and you weren't the priority. And it felt bad.[1]

It's important to note here that even the best, most attuned parents aren't always attuned and attentive. They can't always amplify joy or help you return to joy. A "good enough" parent is more often tuned in to you than missing your signals. They are more often living from a state of connection than from protection. But a Jungle parent is more often living from protection than from connection. Whether because of their own defaults and attachment history or because of difficult circumstances in their lives, their focus is generally on surviving being a parent more than on attuning to the world of their children.

In the Jungle, sometimes your parents had boundaries. They told you what the boundaries were and held you to them. There was structure and things made sense. But sometimes they had no boundaries. You crossed one and they didn't care. Or you crossed a boundary you weren't even aware of and they got mad at you. And they crossed your boundaries, and it hurt and made you mad. It was hard for you to make sense of the interactions.

In a real jungle, things can change fast. The weather can go from good to bad to great. Pretty flowers can hide stinging predators, and majestic rivers can become roaring rapids. In the Jungle of Anxiety, your delights and dangers are just as unpredictable. A parent might be attuned to intimacy, or maybe not. A parent might encourage your small attempts at independence, but later you are punished for them. One moment they were delighted in you, and the next they were done with you.

And so you adapted to the Jungle. You learned how to survive. Slowly the Jungle outside you became the Jungle inside you.

As a little scientist, you ran experiments and collected data on how the Jungle works. Your data kept confirming that there were few reliable rules or patterns in the Jungle. And you found that words and promises were often misleading. What you discovered as a little scientist was that the best way to find small pockets of joyful connection and relief from distress was to focus on other people. You learned to watch closely, to read people. You became an expert in processing social and emotional information. This expertise became your specific strategy for protecting and connecting in the Jungle of Anxiety.

The Yellow Light of Hypervigilance

If you grew up in the Jungle, your attachment defaults are shaped by a *maybe.*

The first default involves the availability of your people. Your people were inconsistently available. When you ask the question, *Is someone available when I am in distress?* the answer comes back as *maybe*. This affects your answer to the second default question, *Will this distress be alleviated?* Again, your answer is *maybe*: *If someone is available to me, maybe my distress will be alleviated. If no one is available, it probably won't be.* Your unconscious conclusions sound something like this:

- *Maybe they will help me when I cry* (pursuing intimacy). *Maybe not.*
- *Maybe they will celebrate what I did* (practicing independence). *Maybe not.*
- *Maybe they will play with me* (intimacy and independence). *Maybe not.*
- *Maybe I will have a joyful connection. Maybe not.*

After countless interactions and experiences, your implicit memory system began to expect this *maybe*. So you started to optimize and manage your life around it.

Maybe functioned as a yellow light embedded in your nervous system. Think of driving. At a yellow light, sometimes you hit the gas to speed up and sometimes you hit the brakes to stop. Sometimes you race toward intimacy. Sometimes you slam on the brakes. Over time this constant speeding up and slowing down—trying to catch up to a positive relational situation or avoid a negative one—became wired in your nervous system as *hypervigilance*. The only way to experience joyful connection was to be constantly watching and waiting so that you would know when the time was right and when it was wrong.

Because of this sense of living in response to the people around you, you grew up feeling little sense of agency. This is because you used your agency to respond to other people (intimacy) rather than to take action (independence). Always watching the yellow light directed your focus outside yourself. Your agency was deployed to protect yourself by staying intimate with your people.

As you were always trying to decide whether to speed up or slam on the brakes, you became extremely focused on your social, emotional, and relational environment. You became expertly attentive to others, how they were feeling and acting in the present, how they might feel and act in the future. If you were raised in the Jungle of Anxiety, you actually sense the coming and going of emotion expressed through the face quicker than other people.[2]

You became a mind reader. An empath. A socioemotional detective. You followed all the clues hiding under the words and promises, disguised as facial expressions, tone of voice, and body posture. You became hypervigilant in tracking whatever might lead to joyful connection and avoiding everything that might cause abandonment.

All this hypervigilance comes with a big dose of anxiety. Anxiety about where your people are. Anxiety about how your relationships are doing. Anxiety about whether you are doing all the right things for all the different relationships.

Because you are scattered among these relationships, you develop skills for surviving in the Jungle, skills to manage all the anxiety.

Jungle Survival Skills

You adapt to an environment when you live there long enough. The landscape teaches you what to pay attention to and what to ignore. It trains you on what to approach and what to avoid. You learn to survive.

If you are raised in the Jungle of Anxiety, you develop four major survival skills. You have more than these, but these are the most common. These survival skills generally focus on pursuing intimacy at the expense of practicing independence.[3]

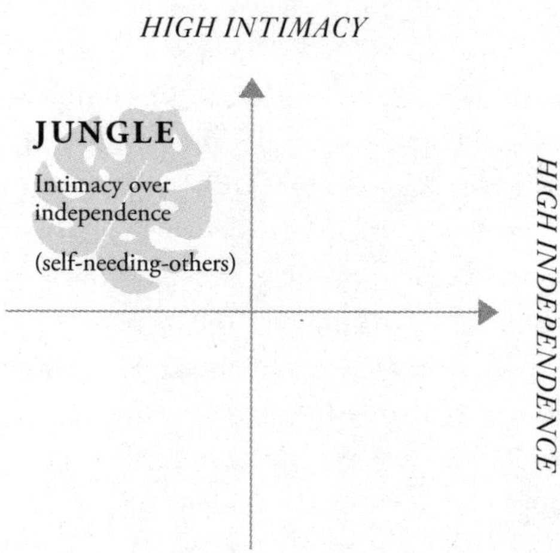

#1. Nonverbal Processing

Life in the Jungle changes fast, but words are slow.

In the Jungle, where relationships and emotions are constantly shifting, you learned to read nonverbal cues. Because people's words didn't always match their actions, you learned to focus on their nonverbal communication. You became an expert in processing all the social-emotional information flowing from your parents, siblings, and others.

To this day, you are a master at noticing what people around you are experiencing. You know when they are saying one thing but mean something else. You are skilled in picking up on body language, tones of voice, and facial expressions. You decipher the subtle relational information to the point that it's louder to you than the words people use. You read bodies, and it is almost like you are reading minds.

Abigail was an incredible boss. Her employees felt seen, known, understood, supported, and encouraged. Abigail treated the people who worked for her like they were her family. She could tell when someone wasn't doing well, and she could give them the freedom to take some time off, even if that meant she needed to work harder.

Abigail was also great at reading her two small children. She would linger longer at bedtime when she sensed her little girl needed extra mommy time. Or she would play a game with her little boy when she could tell he was feeling restless.

She was so good at reading people that she couldn't stop it! Relational information was loud and incessant. She knew when someone was not okay, and it was hard for her to be okay if they weren't. She knew when someone was pretending or faking it. And it bothered her. Mia's coldness toward her was intolerable. Even when she couldn't consciously put her finger on it, she could feel it. She absorbed the emotions of others. This is part of the persistent anxiety in the Jungle—always feeling all the feelings in any room.

If you grew up in the Jungle, your brain and body are wired to read nonverbal communication. Your nervous system prioritizes the body language, facial expressions, and tones of voice of people around you. And you unconsciously deprioritize the actual words they are saying and the logical connections they are making.[4]

In the Jungle, words are slow and misleading, but nonverbal cues are fast and accurate. This skill helped you survive.

#2. Relationships over Rules

In the Jungle, the only pattern is that there are no patterns. So you learned to prioritize relationships over rules.

You overlook the small stuff in others so you can stay connected. You don't mind people who are different from you. You're always willing to make exceptions as long as you feel connected. The moment you sense disconnection, you give up your plans or preferences to stay close.

> *As a project manager, Abigail could intuit her clients' personalities and preferences as she listened to them. The ideas she offered were always better than the clients had imagined. Because the relationship with a client was more important than the written contract, she was willing to add small extras and make midstream changes.*
>
> *Abigail is like this because rules and boundaries were inconsistent in her early childhood. She learned she could bend the rules to squeeze out a little more connection time from her parents. She also learned that people might break their promises and fail to be there for her. Sometimes she would bend or break her own boundaries to stay connected. In Abigail's unconscious mind, she could not have healthy boundaries and pursue connection at the same time.*

In the Jungle, the only rule was to pursue relationships. This skill helped you survive. It helped you manage the anxiety.

#3. Going to Your People

In the Jungle, where relationships are everything, you go to your people for help.

When you are in distress, overwhelmed, confused, or depressed, your default is to go to your people. Because the Jungle has no rules that you can learn and follow on your own, you didn't develop a sense of individual agency. So now you struggle to practice independence. You use others to coregulate your emotions when you are overwhelmed and can't regulate them by yourself (which feels like all the time). Your only option is to pursue intimacy when you are overwhelmed, distressed, or dysregulated. The result of growing up in the Jungle is that you don't trust your own problem-solving ability (your agency) and instead default to pursuing proximity with others.

Because of her Jungle skills, Abigail was great at connecting with people. She had strong relationships with her two small kids, her team of employees, and her husband. She talked to her mom or her sister almost every day. Whenever she was upset or feeling uncertain, she would turn to one of these people. She needed to talk it through. She needed to feel heard. She needed to have her connections reaffirmed. She could only regulate her emotions by coregulating with others.

This survival skill explains why Abigail struggled when Brandon spent time with Mia. It felt like "her people" weren't there for her. Her go-to strategy for managing her anxiety was to connect with Brandon. But now he wasn't there. He was with Mia instead. The skill that helped her survive in the Jungle as a child was now creating anxiety as an adult.

Because you have to be so responsive to your social-emotional environment in the Jungle, it's hard to have any sense of your "self" apart from the people you are always watching. You are likely to feel like bits of you are walking around in the bodies of the people you're attached to. When they're okay, you're okay. When they're not okay, you're not okay. Your sense of self is scattered among your relationships. This plays into default #3, *How do I use my agency?* Since you are a self-needing-others, you need your people to help you regulate your emotions and relieve your distress, so you use your agency to maintain connection with them. This is why relationships are always the priority over the rules.

#4. Blaming Yourself

In the Jungle, when something goes wrong, you blame yourself.

The Jungle trained you to be hypervigilant about all your relationships, and these relationships didn't follow clear rules. This eventually turned into the feeling that you are *responsible* for how everyone is doing all the time.

If something is wrong with someone, then it must be your fault. *You* didn't read their nonverbal communication properly (skill #1). *You* didn't prioritize the relationship enough (skill #2). *You* missed that someone needed "their people" (which is, of course, you) and felt abandoned (skill #3). Eventually you start blaming yourself for everything that goes wrong in a relationship. You apologize for things you didn't do and couldn't have known. You give up and give in during arguments. It is easier to take the blame than to bear the disconnection.

> *Abigail was great at recognizing when something was wrong in her relationships. She would then apologize for it.* I should have known better, *she would tell herself.* I should have seen that it was a bad time to bring it up. *Abigail didn't know how to connect to Mia, who always seemed cold and distant toward her. She assumed it was her fault. It left her angry and anxious that she couldn't figure out a relationship with her husband's daughter. She had always been able to figure out how to connect with people in the past.*

Taking the blame leads back to connection. It helped you survive in the Jungle.

The Cost of the Jungle

So far, you can see the ways that Jungle strategies might not always be great for the Jungle dweller. You might be finding that you identify with Abigail. You feel some of the same frustrations or anxieties that Abigail experiences.

Because you maximize intimacy, you are not as independent as you might need to be. You rely heavily on other people.

You are incredibly skilled at reading nonverbals, but you tend to miss cognitive information. Reason, logic, and rules didn't serve you in the Jungle, and so you don't pay as much attention to them.

You are probably exhausted. Being hypervigilant takes a big toll on your body. Your nervous system is often in a low-level state of fight-or-flight, perceiving a constant background threat to connections with your people. This is why you tend to feel reactive rather than able to respond thoughtfully. Constant readiness quickly translates into weariness.

You might tend to be dramatic or extreme. In the Jungle, the environment is so loud and there's so much going on that the only way you'll get noticed is if you're louder and brighter than everything else. You learned to "ramp it up" when you needed something. You might have been called dramatic or hypersensitive, accused of making a big deal out of things that are not. You internalize that you're "too much."

This hypervigilance can also cause you to "hallucinate" rejection. You are so clued in to the nonverbal state of others that you might perceive their hunger as anger, their exhaustion as disinterest, or their indifference as disgust. You read more into the nonverbals than what is actually there.

The Gifts of the Jungle

But before you grow too discouraged, let's notice all the good things you can bring out of the attachment Jungle. No matter how intense your jungle environment—whether in childhood or in your present life—you gain some beautiful gifts from living there. And these gifts, when moving toward secure attachment with God and within the family of the church, become incredible strengths when used in partnership with God's desire to flourish the world.

Abigail's ability to connect with people allows her to understand and even anticipate what they need—which serves her as a business owner with client relationships. Each client feels like they are receiving individualized attention. They feel like they are not being compared to anyone else—because they aren't. In Abigail's mind, each relationship is unique.

Creativity and spontaneity are some of Abigail's gifts as well. She can think outside the box and come up with creative solutions—not only as a business owner but as a parent and a friend. She is willing to be flexible with other people's ideas because relationships are more important to her than the project or the activity.

Jungle dwellers are a gift to the church as well. The Abigails of the world notice when there's tension in the room, when someone feels uncomfortable, when there is an unspoken conflict or unvoiced hurt. For those raised in the Jungle, drawing people out and helping them feel cared for and connected is second nature. They are also willing to overlook outside appearances or behaviors that others might be quick to judge, making them more willing to move toward social outcasts.

Jungle dwellers are people-focused, relationally driven, and sensitive to social dynamics. Since each person is unique, they seek to uncover each person's story. Their gifts bear great fruit in any community.

Anxious Faith and the Jungle God

Against our best intentions and conscious thoughts, however, if we have distorted defaults because of being raised in the Jungle, then we will have a distorted view of God. Our jungle life will create a Jungle god, and our anxious faith will deploy jungle survival skills.

Because Abigail's defaults—her mental models of others, herself, and the world—were formed in the Jungle, she also perceived God to be a Jungle god. The uncertainty of God's availability caused Abigail to live out her faith in sporadic ways. She craved intimacy with God but often unconsciously hesitated to approach God because she feared rejection. She connected most with God in worship songs and in feeling experiences. Imaginative exercises appealed to her, and she loved embodied practices. But she found it difficult to practice these on her own. She thrived when doing them together with me (Cyd) because of the connection with another person.

Nonverbal Processing

When Abigail tried to find a church, she would evaluate churches and worship experiences by how she felt, by how the nonverbal parts connected (or didn't connect) with her. Did she sense God was there? Was the Spirit moving? Beyond the content of the songs or the sermon, was she stirred and inspired? Maybe; maybe not. Did the people seem welcoming? Instead of asking if a church was focused on what is good and true about God or how they practically loved their neighbors, Abigail wanted to feel something. If the feeling wasn't there, then she became bored or judged that God wasn't working there. If the church wasn't exciting like the Jungle, then she thought it probably wasn't a good church to be at.

Together, Abigail and Brandon struggled to find a church because Abigail was always so aware of how Brandon or her kids were experiencing the church that she could hardly notice whether it was a place she could call home or not. She was desperate for community but found it hard not to suspect something under the surface of the greetings she received in each new church they visited. She was suspicious of the childcare workers' smiles as she checked the kids in or picked them up.

Relationships over Rules

Because in the Jungle relationships are always new, exciting, and unpredictable, Abigail would avoid spiritual ruts. Whenever a spiritual discipline or devotional practice seemed to get a little stale, she would switch things up. The rules and patterns of spiritual disciplines were stifling after a while. Raised in the Jungle, she had no category for how rules and regularity could feed a relationship. Her anxious faith pushed her to constantly pursue new things and new experiences to keep her relationship with God "fresh" and "alive."

Sometimes Abigail felt like God was hiding from her. She couldn't quite find the right way to connect with God. She regularly tried whatever practices seemed to be working for her friends or the ideas in the latest book she'd picked up. She loved hearing about God's love and radical hospitality, about how God sees us and knows us. But she would tune out anything about God's rules, expectations, and punishments. She focused on the personal qualities of God and steered clear of commandments.

Going to Your People

In church life, Abigail was seeking deep relationships, community, and intimacy. That is what she would say if you asked her. But what she really needed—like all of us—was to know people would be there when she needed them. But because she grew up in the Jungle, she had no sense of what a healthy boundary was. So if people in a church kept healthy boundaries, Abigail interpreted it as a sign that they were not available, that she didn't belong, that she wasn't wanted. If people didn't drop everything to help her when she needed it (as she did for others), then she would feel rejected and a little bitter. After a while she would wonder if she needed better friends or a new small group. Her anxious faith might judge a healthy church with healthy boundaries as lacking in love and acceptance.

Blaming Yourself

When Abigail couldn't connect with God, she blamed herself. Maybe she wasn't praying with enough intensity or faith, or she wasn't doing enough to get quiet and be present to God. She often carried guilt for not doing enough to stay connected with God, like she was letting God down. If she hadn't turned to God in a while (even a few days), she wondered if God still loved her. Maybe Jesus was mad at her or would reject her because she wasn't paying enough attention—she wasn't loving God with her *entire* heart, soul, mind, and strength. Maybe God wanted to be with her, but maybe not. Maybe God would be available; maybe not. Her anxious faith had turned the God of steadfast and enduring love into the Jungle god of "he loves me, he loves me not."

If you were raised in the Jungle, you can probably relate to Abigail's difficulties in staying connected to God. The permanent *maybe* lodged in your brain and body makes it difficult to feel any confidence or stability with God or God's people. This is what an anxious faith feels like. This is life with a Jungle god.

Thankfully, there is hope for all those who live from the Jungle of Anxiety. God is leading you into the peaceful Pasture. But maybe the Jungle of Anxiety doesn't describe you. In the next chapter, we will explore what survival skills you may have learned in the Desert of Avoidance.

Reflection

What ideas about the Jungle were helpful to you in this chapter?

To what extent do you identify with the description of growing up in a jungle? How did reading this chapter increase your compassion for yourself or someone you know who might have grown up in the Jungle?

Which of the survival strategies do you see yourself or someone you know using? How have they helped or hindered your connections with others, God, or even yourself?

What gifts of the Jungle do you see in yourself or others? How might seeing that there are gifts as well as obstacles increase your compassion for yourself or others?

Try making a jungle picture in a medium of your choice (draw, paint, collage, sculpture, digital, etc.). Fill the picture with detail all the way to all the edges. What emotions do you notice as you keep adding more detail? What does this help you notice about what life in the attachment Jungle might feel like?

Try having a conversation with Jesus about what you've resonated with in this chapter.

CHAPTER 6

DESERT GOD: AN AVOIDANT FAITH

James explained to me (Cyd) that he had never had anything close to an emotive, relational experience of God. He thought of his faith in a very cognitive way. God had his allegiance—that was what it meant to follow Jesus. He was reading a spiritual disciplines book with a group at church but hadn't done any of the practices. He had been told by a pastor friend that he should work on cultivating a deeper, more emotionally connected relationship with God. James had no idea how.

At the same time, James lamented the difference in how his kids related to him compared to the way they related to his wife. He saw their closeness and recognized that he didn't seem capable of that kind of connection. Whenever he got stressed or overwhelmed, he would take off and read a book. He thought it was the way he was wired. But now he was wondering if it wasn't just the easy way out. Maybe he was avoiding the hard work of relationships.

The Desert

Imagine a desert. Life is just barely holding on.

A desert is void of any visible signs of life. Sand dunes and bare rocks stretch in every direction. There's no water in sight, no shade to be found, and the heat rising from the sand is almost as intense as the heat from the sun.

The colors are muted. Everything is a shade of brown or beige, with maybe a hint of red or white. There's not a lot of variety. Everything looks and feels the same.

And it's quiet. Painfully quiet. No singing birds, no buzzing insects, no rustling leaves, and no rushing water. Silence.

Except for the wind, whipping and howling and turning grains of sand into sharp knives that tear at your skin and torment your eyes. The only way to survive is to make sure every inch of your body is covered, to hide from the sun, to guard against the cutting wind. To survive, you must find and protect water, stay in the shade, and only move around when necessary, preferably in the cooler parts of the day. To survive, you must follow the rules and patterns of the land. Any exceptions could be deadly. The desert is desolate, forbidding, forsaken, devoid of life.

Maybe you grew up in a relational environment like a desert. Emotional affirmation and acceptance were sparse. They had to be protected and defended. Emotional rejection and abandonment were as harsh as the desert sun, and so your movements had to be carefully planned so you didn't get burned. In such an environment it makes sense that your survival strategy is primarily to withdraw and conserve, to be distanced and reserved—from others and even from yourself. It makes sense that you feel like you have to control your relational and emotional environment. It makes sense that you feel like it is all up to you.

Growing Up in the Desert

Where does the attachment Desert come from?

The attachment Desert comes from caregiving that regularly

rejects social and emotional connection. Maybe your parents cared for your physical needs, helped with your schoolwork, and showed up for your games or concerts, but they ignored, pulled away, or punished you for having emotional needs. They disappeared when the deep things started to appear. Maybe your caregivers didn't know how to handle their own emotions, and so didn't know what to do with yours. Maybe they were raised to ignore their own emotions and desires for connection, so your emotions and desires were invisible to them. Either way, you felt dismissed and rejected.

This relational distance was also expressed as physical distance. You weren't physically held, hugged, or cuddled as often as other kids. Maybe you were placed in a crib alone when your parents felt you were crying too much. Maybe you had to play by yourself so you didn't bother anyone.

Their rejection of your bids for connection created a deep-seated feeling of abandonment. Their dismissive negative emotions caused you to learn to hide. And their praise for following the rules (the only times you got positive emotional connection from them) taught you to perform.

Your caregivers would think and say it was good for you to have a consistent structure, and they praised you for being so independent. But really, it was good for them. That was probably how they were avoiding and dismissing their own anxieties.

Your caregivers had strict boundaries, and they couldn't be bothered to change them for you. You had to fit inside their boundaries, rules, and routines. When you did, you got the positive emotional connection you desired (even if you slowly stopped admitting to yourself that you desired connection at all). But when you didn't fit into the rules and routines, didn't meet or exceed expectations, or your emotions came out too much and too big, you were dismissed, rejected, and put to the side again. And that hurt.

You were raised in an emotional desert. Relational and emotional connection was a scarce resource. Like conserving water in the desert, you had to follow strict rules for getting and keeping minimal relational connection. Don't expect too much, or you will be disappointed. Don't break the rules, or it will evaporate.

You stopped hoping for abundant connection with others. You started trusting mostly in yourself. You got really good at solving your own problems. You were even praised for being so independent and self-reliant. You paid attention to rules, expectations, and routines. You ignored emotions, your body, and the emotions and bodies of other people.

And slowly, the Desert outside became the Desert within.

When I asked James more about his life up to this point, he described growing up in a household where all his physical needs were met. He had all the signs of a stable life. He had food on the table, a house to live in, and parents who supported him in his schoolwork and provided what looked like a very strong start to his life.

But emotions weren't talked about in his house. He learned early on that his internal world was unimportant. What mattered was measurable on the outside.

Because he was raised in a Christian home and knew faith was important, he developed strong spiritual practices. He read and studied his Bible regularly. He loved God's Word so much that he went to seminary and entered into pastoral ministry. But even in his ministry contexts, he found that his emotions were unimportant. Truth reigned supreme. What people felt didn't matter.

The Red Light of the Desert

Is someone available to me when I'm in distress?

While those in the Jungle of Anxiety live with a *maybe*, people living in the Desert of Avoidance receive a *no*.

- *No, they won't respond when I cry or express other emotions* (pursuing intimacy).
- *No, they won't celebrate what I did* (practicing independence), *unless I did what they wanted within their expectations.*

- *No, they don't really play and get silly with me* (intimacy and independence).
- *No, I don't have joyful connection. I feel tolerated, and my anger about it eventually turned my insides into a barren desert. I don't feel much anymore.*

After regular interactions and experiences growing up, your implicit memories about how relationships work and your nervous system's shifts between connection and protection were shaped by this no. As an infant, a child, an adolescent, and an adult, this no was internalized as painful rejection and emotional abandonment. So you started to organize your life around avoiding that pain and distancing yourself from those feelings of rejection and abandonment.

This no functioned as a red light embedded in your nervous system. Unlike the relational speeding up and slowing down caused by the yellow light of hypervigilance that eventually grew into life in the Jungle, avoiding the pain of rejection and abandonment pushed you toward always slowing down, stopping, using caution, staying distant. And this slowly grew into the Desert of Avoidance.

Because you lived at a distance from others and from yourself, under the sun of abandonment and with relational springs of water few and far between, you developed skills for surviving in the Desert, skills at maintaining avoidance.

Desert Survival Skills

Every environment teaches you what to pay attention to and what to ignore, what information to prioritize and what information to discard, what to approach and what to avoid. You learn to survive in the landscape you were raised in.

To survive in the Desert, you developed four major survival skills (which are almost opposite of those necessary in the Jungle). These survival skills generally focus on practicing independence at the expense of pursuing intimacy.[1]

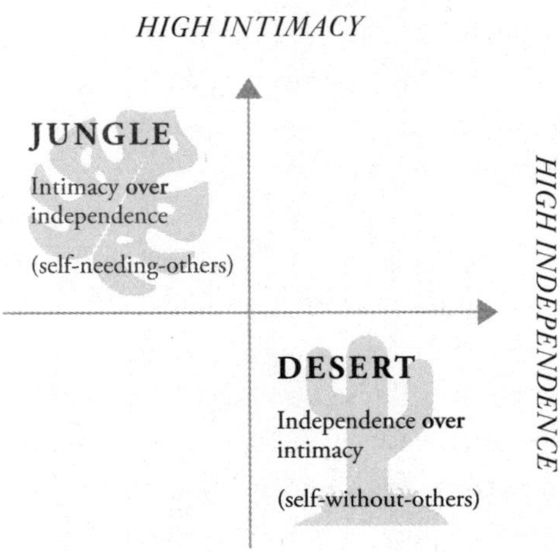

#1. Logical-Linear Processing

Life in the Desert is slow and deliberate. Accuracy is required.

In the Desert, where relationships are dry and emotions are buried, you learned to plan on what is predictable. You prioritized what is logical and linear. You concentrated on cause and effect and finding the mechanisms between them. You became a master at processing patterns about the relational environment so that you could avoid the burning sun of abandonment and find your way between the meager springs of water. Your body and your brain learned to prioritize rational, verbal, logical, and linear information. And your nervous system started ignoring emotional and nonverbal information because it was rare and often dangerous.[2]

To this day, you like to master the meaning of words, find logical connections, and solve cognitive problems.

Unlike those raised in the Jungle, who are experts at nonverbal and emotional communication, you excel at verbal and rational communication. Neuroscientists have even observed that those with a Desert attachment strategy will look at the mouth when someone is talking to them instead of looking at their eyes the way Jungle dwellers do.[3]

And it isn't even accurate to say that you are ignoring nonverbal communication. You actually don't see it, don't notice it. Your body and brain don't value that kind of information and now bypass and discard it.

> *James was incredibly skilled here. He was a deep thinker and an excellent problem solver. He was the guy who could figure things out. He could think clearly when others were confused. He could remain calm in chaos and crisis. He kept his head when others' emotions ran high. He was the one who could rise above whatever crisis or conflict was happening and see the bigger picture. He could see the deeper theological questions beneath the turmoil and speak truth in the midst of confusion. His survival strategy was a gift to his community.*
>
> *However, when someone was upset about something, James couldn't see it. No matter how big the hints, the only way James would find out someone was upset was if they directly confronted him.*

In the Desert, emotions are dangerous and unpredictable. But cause and effect and logical connections keep you alive. This skill helps you survive.

#2. Rules over Relationships

In the Desert, everything works on a schedule, has a pattern, and is predictable. So you learned to prioritize rules over relationships.

You are good at following explicit rules and spoken expectations. You find safety in doing things the right way at the right time for the right reasons. You look for patterns in words, behaviors, and events, then use those patterns to make your plans—plans that usually emphasize independence over intimacy.

You believe that if people could just develop clear rules—and everyone would actually follow them—life would be better because it would be predictable. After all, routines reduce anxiety, so let's all follow the routines and rules.

> *James was good at seeing patterns. This made him effective in his church because he could regularly remind people of the patterns of God's story and encourage people to remain faithful.*

But all the while, James noticed another pattern that was harder for him to talk about. He saw a series of tragedies God had not prevented. There had been sudden losses within his church community and even in his own family. He saw the pattern of suffering. In this way, the ability to see the pattern was making it difficult for James to trust God. Cognitively, he could explain how suffering could produce fruitfulness and strength in God's people. But relationally, the pattern made it difficult to trust God.

In the Desert, relationships are unreliable and emotions are unpredictable. So you follow the rules and create routines to survive. This skill helps you survive the relationally harsh environment.

#3. Doing It Yourself

In the Desert, where relationships are unreliable, you learned to do everything yourself.

When you are stressed, overwhelmed, upset, or facing a problem, your default is to do it yourself. You can figure it out. You can muscle through it. You are independent, resourceful, competent, and creative. You take action, figure it out, and make it happen. Because you see the patterns and know the rules, you know how to solve problems—and you get frustrated when people just want to *talk about* the problem. *Let's just fix it!* you think when others are talking about it.

Growing up, when you were dysregulated and distressed, you were most often left alone to figure it out, or you were actively shamed for expressing negative emotions. So you learned to fend for yourself, to do it yourself. You learned to practice independence. And you learned not to pursue intimacy.

You hate to ask for help, for three reasons. First, on the surface, you don't think to ask for help because you know what to do. You see yourself as a competent problem solver. You'll just figure it out or tough it out. Second, a little deeper, you don't ask for help because you believe that people are generally unhelpful. It will be quicker and better to do it yourself. Third, deep down, you don't want to admit that you need help. You don't want to show your vulnerable side because then, if people don't help or don't respond well, you will have to feel the hurt of rejection and abandonment again—and deep down, you vowed never to feel that way again. But of course, the problem is that each time you do it yourself, the Desert within grows bigger and stronger.

> *James was someone who got things done. He didn't need to wait around for permission or direction. If he saw a problem or an issue, he would move into action. He wasn't the kind of guy who needed to be recognized or given credit, so his work wasn't always noticed. But when his community faced tragedies, James was the one who could keep functioning. He knew what needed to happen, and he kept things afloat. He knew it wasn't a great idea to rely on other people to contribute, and he was willing to step in and do it himself. He rarely even noticed this was what he was doing. He didn't consciously report that he didn't trust other people or that he thought people wouldn't help. He just didn't ask. He did it himself.*
>
> *At some point during our conversations, James made the comment, "I've learned that it's probably a good idea not to rely on God too much." From the pattern of suffering and tragedy he had traced, he had come to assume that he was pretty much on his own.*

In the Desert, doing it yourself is faster, better, and, most importantly, safer. Practicing independence is a defense against pursuing intimacy.

#4. Blaming Others

In the Desert, when something goes wrong, you blame others.

This is the culmination of the previous Desert survival skills. If something is wrong with you, others, or the world, or if stress is being added to your life (or anyone around you), it is *clearly* not your fault.

Why?

Because you are logical and linear, and you communicate clearly and directly—or so you think (skill #1). You are doing your best to follow the rules that help manage stress and keep things under control (skill #2). And when things become unmanageable, you kick into gear and do it yourself (skill #3). So if things are still falling apart, if you or others are losing their cool (pushing beyond the window of tolerance), then *clearly* others are to blame!

> *Even though James worked hard to maintain a gracious and generous posture toward others, he was also able to admit that he spent a lot of time frustrated and disappointed with others. People were less committed than he thought they should be to whatever work they were called to. At one point, he was able to express great regret about the way he had criticized his wife in their early years of marriage. "I thought the problem was her, but it turns out it was me."*

In the Desert, blaming others accomplishes two things. First, blaming others places you at a distance from them—which is kind of how you like it (this is what the Desert does). And second, blaming others protects your image of yourself as competent and independent, that you don't really need other people because they are the ones messing everything up. Because deep down you already feel rejected by people, you can reassure yourself that you are right to keep your distance because they are always to blame.

The Cost of the Desert

So far, you can see the ways that Desert strategies might not always be great for the Desert dweller. You might find that you feel some of the same frustrations or anxieties that James experiences.

Because you maximize independence, you do not pursue intimacy as frequently as you might need to. You rely heavily on yourself.

You are incredibly skilled in cognitive and logical information, but you miss nonverbal cues. Reason, logic, and rules are so important to you that you might end up hurting the people in your life. You may be technically right but relationally wrong.

You conserve your energy. Relationships with others take work, and you might find it draining to communicate with those close to you. You need to know when a conversation is going to turn relational so you can gear yourself up for it. You're probably ready for the conversation to end long before the other person and will leave exhausted by the relational toll it took.

You might hold other people at arm's length, careful not to expose yourself or let others get too close. If you think back to the desert, the environment is so sparse and there's so little going on that the only way you'll survive is to plan ahead and pace yourself. You learned to fend for yourself when you needed something rather than relying on others. You might have been called distant or insensitive, accused of not caring enough or being out of touch with emotions.

You can also tend to miss bids for connection from your people even when they're trying to be clear. You're so unpracticed in noticing nonverbals that you might miss the smiles of encouragement and the touches of affection and perceive people moving toward you as cramping your space. You might perceive that no one wants to connect with you because you're missing the signs people are giving you.

You might feel a little like a "bodiless mind." Your nervous system rarely detects what's going on in your body. You were never taught to pay attention to your internal world, including the cues your body might be giving you about what you're feeling.

> *When James started learning to practice awareness of his body, he slowly noticed every part of his body from head to toe and paid attention to sensations in each part. He was surprised to discover that he almost always carried tension in his jaw and restlessness in his arms when he wanted to withdraw. As he began to pick up on these signals, he was able to recognize how he was being critical of his environment and resisting his circumstances. His body had been trying to tell him for years that he needed to change his ways, but he couldn't pick up on the signals because he lived in his mind.*

The Gifts of the Desert

But before you grow too discouraged, notice all the good things you can bring out of the attachment Desert. No matter how barren your

Desert is—whether in childhood or your present life—you gain some beautiful gifts from living there. And these gifts, when moving toward secure attachment with God and within the family of the church, become incredible strengths when used in partnership with God's desire to flourish the world.

In whatever communities he finds himself, James is a stabilizing force. Because he is capable and competent, people can count on him to do what he says he will do. He lends structure and consistency to work and worship. He is thoughtful when making decisions and sticks to the decisions he makes. Surprisingly, Desert dwellers can also be great listeners when they turn listening into a task to accomplish. Because they don't get wrapped up in other people's emotions, they can be quite good at listening to someone talk and then offering helpful insight into the problem.

James is a strategic thinker and holds the course to reach the goal, even when it feels scary. Because of his integrity and ability to see the big picture, he made excellent decisions to help cast the vision of the organization to other people who were nervous about results. His focus and consistency helped move things forward.

Desert dwellers can often see the principles that are operating underneath the surface. They can identify the root causes of problems rather than getting caught up in addressing symptoms. They can see that an extremely gifted person isn't in the right place or that someone in leadership doesn't have the skills they need. They can think objectively about process and performance because they don't get caught up in relational dynamics or favoritism.

Desert dwellers are a huge gift to churches! Because they can focus on facts, they can offer realistic observations about the current condition of a church. Desert dwellers can make excellent church consultants because they can assess the parts, see the whole picture, and offer excellent ideas for aligning the church with its mission. Desert dwellers can not only think strategically and stay focused on the mission of God, they can also see clearly when a ministry is limping along and might need to be released in order to reprioritize the resources elsewhere. Because they don't get emotionally involved in particular ministries, they are able to see what's not aligned with the mission, even if it's a tradition.

Avoidant Faith and the Desert God

Against our best intentions and conscious thoughts, if we have distorted defaults because of being raised in the Desert, then we will have a distorted view of God. Our Desert life will create a Desert god, and our avoidant faith will deploy Desert survival skills.

Because James's attachment defaults—his mental models of others, himself, and the world—were formed in the Desert, deep down he perceives God as also living in the Desert. God is a Desert god, and James practices an avoidant faith. God is the God of rules, order, and sovereign independence over and beyond creation. God's will must be followed. Two things are needed for following God's will: knowing it and doing it. Thankfully, reason and willpower (knowing and doing) are what Desert dwellers are good at. For James, because God doesn't feel available and doesn't really offer intimacy, he focuses instead on studying Scripture and being obedient to God. James feels closest to God through the intellectual side of faith and by serving others—though James doesn't really speak of being close to God.

Logical-Linear Processing

Of course faith has a bit of mystery. But the mystery should still make sense. God's ways are higher than our ways, so it is reasonable that God doesn't always seem reasonable to us. The Bible might not always seem believable, but that's because there is a deeper logic that we need in order to understand it. At least, that is what James thinks. He prefers a church that explains the reasonableness, coherence, and logic of faith. Maybe James didn't always like what theologians came up with, but if it sounded reasonable, then he would agree with it.

After moving to a new city, James was looking for a church that preached the truth of the Bible, not merely inspirational messages. He wanted to know about their doctrinal positions, and he might even ask about their bylaws. James wasn't interested in a touchy-feely small group where people shared their lives. He would much rather sign up for a Bible study that was really going to dig into the Word.

Rules over Relationships

Because rules are more important than relationships in the Desert, James would distance himself from those with different theological beliefs. He valued doctrinal purity over church unity. On a personal level, James tried to do what the church expected of him when it came to giving and serving (except the idea that everyone should be in a small group). Spiritually, James was pretty up and down with his prayer life, and he hated most devotional books because they were too shallow. But he would listen to a theology or Bible podcast every once in a while, in addition to preparing sermons. Basically, as long as James did his part, then God should do God's part. That's the deal he struck in his heart about his relationship with God.

Doing It Yourself

In the Desert, practicing independence was rewarded, and pursuing intimacy was punished. This means that when you have a problem, you fix it yourself. And if someone else has a problem, you also fix it. Desert dwellers are experts at using their agency to fix problems—as long as they aren't intimacy problems, which they avoid and ignore.

While he didn't know it and would deny it if you asked him, James lived by the mantra that Christians should always help others but never ask for help. He would help people move, throw in some extra money to help a family fix their car, and show up for the church workday to help clean up the property. But he wouldn't admit that finances were tight, ask for prayer when he had that cancer scare, or show weakness or vulnerability. James certainly wouldn't admit when he had doubts.

Blaming Others

Because Desert dwellers follow the rules and do it themselves, they aren't the ones to blame when something goes wrong. Others are to blame. If people do bad things, then God will punish them for it. If they do good things, God will reward them.

Of course, Desert dwellers include God in this logic too. When his best friend died unexpectedly, leaving a young family behind, James blamed God. James knew his friend was doing everything right, trying his best to love God and others. It wasn't fair that God took him. Publicly, James knew God was sovereign and people should submit to God's will. But privately, James felt God wasn't playing by the rules and resented God for it. It all just reinforced the idea that God was distant and uninterested in him.

Those raised in the Desert feel a cosmic *no* from God—*No, God is not available!* This no, lodged in their brain and body, makes it so difficult to hope for a deep relationship with God or God's people. It is safer to keep a bit of distance, safer to trust God with their might but not be vulnerable with their heart.

It is safer to have an avoidant faith and believe in a Desert god.

Thankfully, there is hope for all those who live from the Desert of Avoidance. God wants to lead Desert dwellers into the Pasture of deeper connection, where both intimacy and independence thrive together.

Reflection

What ideas about the Desert were helpful to you in this chapter?

To what extent do you identify with the description of growing up in a Desert? How did reading this chapter increase your compassion for yourself or for someone you know who might have grown up in the Desert?

Which of the survival strategies do you see yourself or someone you know using? How have they helped or hindered your connections with others, God, or even yourself?

What gifts of the Desert do you see in yourself or others? How might seeing that there are gifts as well as obstacles increase your compassion for yourself or others?

Try making a desert picture in a medium of your choice (pencil, ink, paint, collage, sculpture, digital, etc.). Focus on the simplicity, the scarcity of resources, the lack of life. What emotions do you notice as you resist adding more detail? What does this help you notice about what life in an attachment Desert might feel like?

Try having a conversation with Jesus about what you've resonated with in this chapter.

CHAPTER 7

WAR ZONE GOD: A CHAOTIC FAITH

Now that we've explored the Jungle and the Desert, it's time to take a look at the War Zone.

Before we do, we want to be very clear. If you find yourself in the War Zone, we want to affirm the amount of healing work you have already done in your life to be able to get this many chapters in! Thank you for trusting us enough to keep reading.

Based on conversations with people who have met Jesus in the War Zone and moved toward the Pasture, we are sharing a composite of their stories in this chapter because we want you to know that you're not alone. Each of the people who shared their stories with us is making significant movement toward the Pasture and meeting Jesus in new and radically healing ways. Your story may be very different from the ones shared here. What you'll likely recognize in their stories and in your own is the pervasive fear that lurks beneath the surface of your life.

How could this fear not carry over into your relationship with God and your interactions in church communities? Finding a church that feels safe can be incredibly difficult for you. Because of the conflicted nature of your attachments, it's hard for you to believe the words and trust the actions of other people.

It's not your fault. Growing up with erratic joy and confusing experiences of intimacy and independence leaves you with fearful defaults that make it hard to find your footing and cause you to behave in ways that are confusing and frustrating to you and to the people around you. But it needn't stay this way.

It is our hope that this chapter will do one of two things for you.

First, if you find yourself in the War Zone, we hope this chapter will give you greater compassion for yourself and language to help others understand you. Because of the complexity and uniqueness of each person's experience, we recognize that reading a chapter in a book will not be all you need, but we want it to be a compassionate beginning for you. It is likely you will benefit from the growth pathways we suggest for the Jungle and the Desert in part 3, especially if practiced in conjunction with care from a trauma-informed therapist or spiritual director.

Second, if you are not in the War Zone, we hope that this basic understanding of the War Zone will give you greater compassion for your brothers and sisters who have grown up there. We hope you will be more able to connect with those in the War Zone and less likely to blame, shame, or villainize them. They need you to have the capacity to be a new family for them, and they have much to offer you along their journey of healing. They are brave survivors.

The Freezer or the Fire

When Ashley got home from school, her mom had already finished half a bottle of wine. When her mom finished that one, she would retire upstairs to finish another bottle while watching TV and drifting off to sleep before doing it all again the next day. She gave Ashley no hugs, no affection, no nothing. If she expressed anything, it was just the oozing of quiet resentment at Ashley's very existence.

But then her dad would come home from work, full of attention and affection, making dinner, cleaning up a little, and helping Ashley with school. His love covered over a multitude of sins. Her dad's love was like a warm fire that thawed some of the freezer of her mom.

Except when it burned too hot. All that love and affection could also turn to anger and rage. His explosive outbursts felt like they would burn down the house, coming with excessive punishments for minor infractions and physical bruises as reminders. As much as the fire of her dad's affection thawed a frozen heart, it also burned uncontrollably and unpredictably. These fits of rage and abuse blurred the meaning of love.

With a frozen mom and a fiery dad, Ashley learned to keep the peace by keeping secrets. Her parents would be furious if she let anyone know how dysfunctional her family was, and so she learned that lying was a form of loving. In order to have love and affection, she would automatically have to cope with pain and fear. They were inseparable.

Parenting the Parents

Christopher's mom seemed helpless, fragile, and frightened. She would give him exuberant praise and encouragement for the smallest things, but Christopher soon figured out it was all talk—mostly, she wanted to protect herself from any negative experiences or emotions. Whenever a big, unruly emotion showed up in anyone, she disappeared (emotionally and physically). All those fake platitudes and all that toxic positivity taught Christopher he couldn't really trust anything she said. It was just smoke and mirrors.

She always seemed brittle and on the verge of a breakdown. And Christopher's dad made it clear that Christopher was responsible for keeping his mom sane. Christopher couldn't make loud noises because it would upset her. He couldn't express any needs because it would overwhelm her. He couldn't have friends over because it would be just . . . too . . . much!

So Christopher learned how to keep his mom from the brink of breakdown. It was his responsibility to emotionally regulate her, to walk on eggshells, to anticipate problems and needs for her. Instead of her being attuned to his needs and emotions, he was attuned to hers—and was deemed a failure when he wasn't. In her helplessness, he was parenting her.

Christopher had to parent his helpless mother because his father couldn't be bothered to be a loving husband to her. He didn't bother acting like a loving father either. But he demanded the *respect* of a father. And if it wasn't given, there would be consequences.

A hug and a kiss before bed was a sign of respect—even though he never offered the kids any displays of affection. Prompt obedience was a sign of respect. Minding your manners—especially in public—was a sign of respect.

But because Christopher's dad was convinced the world was against him, he saw disrespect everywhere and was easily offended. So he lashed out at every opportunity, directing verbal and physical abuse at the nearest person. The slightest perceived offense or sign of disrespect led to harsh words and the cold shoulder, sometimes even physical reminders.

Because he was a small boy who still wanted to be near his dad, Christopher figured out all his dad's interests. He eventually landed on sports and politics. Even as a child Christopher would read the newspaper: the front page (for politics) and the back page (for sports). With this knowledge, he could engage with—and, if necessary, distract—his dad. Christopher learned which teams to love and who played for them, and which policies to hate and why. Just as he did with his mother, Christopher was attuning to the interests of his dad rather than his dad attuning to Christopher's interests. And Christopher was doing this for protection more than for connection.

Christopher's mom always seemed frightened and helpless, and his dad was frightening and hostile. Christopher kept his mom from the brink of breakdown and braced himself against his dad's blowups.

While desiring connection, he needed protection from his parents. To survive, Christopher was carefully parenting his parents through their breakdowns and blowups.

When kids and adolescents are forced to take on parental roles, it might look the way it did for Christopher. But it can also look like caring for younger siblings, excessive cooking and cleaning, refereeing arguments between the parents, being the public presence for the family, or being an emotional support (acting like a confidant or therapist) for one or both parents, all in developmentally inappropriate ways. This is called *reverse parenting*, or *parentification*, and it comes in various degrees, from mild to abusive.[1]

The War Zone

Imagine a war zone.

Not the aftermath of war, but an active war.

It's a civil war fought between families, friends, and fellow citizens. Bombs are falling. Buildings are crumbling. There are few places to hide. It's hard to distinguish friend from foe, and people keep switching sides. Part of you wants to run and get away, but another part of you wants to stay and fight.

Basic supplies are low, and it feels dangerous to go out for food and water. You are never sure when the next attack will happen. Your body is always tense, always ready, always prepared for immediate action.

And there are land mines—buried under the earth, ready for every misstep. Because of the mines, there are entire parts of the city and surrounding countryside that you never go to.

In a war zone, you do whatever it takes to survive, no matter how jumbled or contradictory the actions might seem. Staying alive is what matters.

Maybe you grew up in a relational environment that was a war zone. The people who were supposed to help you also hurt you. Those who delighted in you were also a danger to you. Your protectors were also the perpetrators. You didn't know if you should approach them or avoid them. You grew up in the War Zone if the people you loved were both the source of and the solution to your distress.

Growing Up in the War Zone

How does the attachment War Zone form?

The War Zone comes from caregiving that is traumatizing and abusive, frightening and fearful, or withdrawn and neglectful. In the War Zone, you regularly receive messages that you are loved and cherished but also hated and despised. You might receive a hug, but you are also hit (whether emotionally or physically).

The War Zone comes from a childhood of attach and defend.

Yes, you read that right. *Attach.*

As a baby who couldn't care for itself, you needed to *attach* to your caretaker. But you also needed to *defend* yourself from them—emotionally and sometimes physically. You tried to seek proximity, but not too close, because that might trigger a bad situation. You tried to keep your distance, but not too far because you still needed care.

We can see this attach and defend in Ashley seeking emotional warmth from her father but also fearing his unpredictable rage. She was always on high alert for any signs that he was about to blow up (defend), but she was also desperate to find any sign that he was ready to connect, that he was pleased or proud of her (attach). Similarly, Christopher mimicked his father's interests (attach) but was constantly bracing against emotional and physical abuse (defend).

Your environment was in conflict, and that caused a contradiction within you. The confusion outside you (*Are my parents good or bad?*) became the confusion within you (*Am I good or bad?*). When you regularly received contradictory messages—in words and deeds—of "Come here!" and "Go away!" or "I delight in you!" and "You disgust me!" you developed contradictory behaviors to survive in this environment. These contradictory messages created disorganized strategies for dealing with life, strategies that seemed to shift without rhyme or reason. You became as unpredictable as your parents, often surprising yourself with your explosive reactions or trembling withdrawal.

These paradoxical messages became internalized as deep fear and shame, often expressed outwardly as anger or rage. You were afraid of those you were supposed to love, and this brought you shame. Because you didn't want to believe the problem was with your caregivers, you assumed it must have been something you did to cause all the problems. You might have also felt ashamed for always feeling afraid. A primary way to temporarily overcome shame was through anger—directed at yourself, at others, or at the world in general. This rage became a short-term solution for enduring powerlessness produced by fear and shame.

Two Sides of Growing Up in the War Zone

The War Zone comes about in two main ways. The first is hostile parenting. The second is helpless parenting.[2]

What is called *hostile and self-referential* parenting is when life is all about the parent—their feelings, priorities, and reactions. These parents do contradictory things like rejecting their children while also seeking their attention, demanding that the child look at them or smile while also insulting or degrading them. While similar to the Jungle environment of inconsistent and intrusive parenting, the War Zone adds active rejection, berating, and emotional or physical abuse or extreme neglect way beyond what folks in the Desert experience. The response of the child is fear of their caregiver, while also internalizing deep shame about themselves.

But the opposite can also happen, where the parent seems frightened of the child. This is called *helpless and fearful* parenting. These parents continually communicate (implicitly and explicitly) that they are overwhelmed and afraid of their own children, acting hesitantly toward them and withdrawing from them. These parents might seem frail, always about to crumble under the responsibility of raising a child, and often give in to the demands of their children without offering any initiative of their own. Helpless parents often express willingness to greet their children but subtly turn them away (rejection) if they get too close.

Parents who doubted or criticized their own ability to care for you would likely send you signals of both fear and disgust. These signals of fear and disgust were then internalized as *I am disgusting* or *People should be afraid of me*. In the environment of helpless parents, "even if caregivers aren't yelling at their children or hitting them or abusing them in some other way, they can be generating enough fear, anger, or chaos in the environment to cause the child's attachment system to shut down."[3] The sad reality is that while hostile parenting might be easier to identify and understand as producing an attachment War Zone, helpless parenting is just as damaging and just as likely to occur.

These contradictory messages are mirrored in the lies between the private life internal to the family and the public face the parents project to the rest of the world. While privately Dad's voice could be angry or Mom's face would flash disgust, the moment a friend called, they stopped yelling and put on a happy face. These rapid shifts in tone of voice and facial expression added to the children's internal confusion, leading to distortion and lies.

The war of your parents' unprocessed trauma and abuse became the war inside you. You internalized contradictory messages about others, yourself, and the world. These messages became a chronic and chaotic sense of feeling afraid, angry, and ashamed.

But you are not disgusting. People do not need to be afraid of you. You do not need to keep yourself from the world or lash out against it. The problem isn't you. It's the defaults that were shaped in you without your awareness.

The Dysfunctional Stoplight of the War Zone

We've talked about how attachment defaults are set to *yes*, *maybe*, or *no* in the other landscapes.

The three words—*yes*, *maybe*, *no*—have a clear meaning. The meaning they create was illustrated through the idea of a relational stoplight.

- *Yes* is like a green light, meaning it is safe to proceed in relationships. It is safe to pursue intimacy and practice independence.
- *Maybe* is like a yellow light, meaning you should speed up or slow down to pursue intimacy while neglecting independence.
- *No* is like a red light, meaning you should stop pursuing intimacy and focus on practicing independence.

But in the War Zone, it's impossible to create consistent meaning because of the nature of the attach-and-defend life you had to navigate. Because everything was always shifting and your caregivers struggled to focus on your well-being, you couldn't create a consistent *yes*, *no*, or *maybe*. It's as if the stoplight is broken.

Clinically, the War Zone is called a *disorganized attachment* because it is impossible for children to make meaning out of the contradictory messages and conflicting behaviors of their parents.[4] The Pasture is organized around both intimacy and independence, the Jungle is organized around prioritizing intimacy, and the Desert is organized around prioritizing independence. But the War Zone vacillates between prioritizing intimacy and independence. It's chaotic and confusing, and it's difficult to find a consistent survival strategy because the environment seems to be actively destroying all your efforts.

But somehow, you survived, and you're reading this book. And that is truly remarkable! We are grateful for your courage to persevere. We hope you might find that you make more sense than you—or others—think you do! You're not crazy or broken beyond repair.

Disorganized Survival Skills: Attach and Defend Parts

Raised in the War Zone, you likely learned some or all of the survival skills found in the Jungle and the Desert. But you learned them in haphazard and contradictory ways (that's why it's called a disorganized attachment). As a little scientist, running experiments about joyful connection and how intimacy and independence work, you tried all sorts of things and learned a wide range of survival skills. You have more variety in your survival skills than people who grew up in only the Jungle or Desert. But your survival skills are often conflicting because you developed highly sensitive attach *and* defend parts within yourself. These parts can rapidly switch back and forth between the opposing survival strategies of the Jungle and the Desert. These attach and defend parts are fragments of yourself all trying to help you survive.[5]

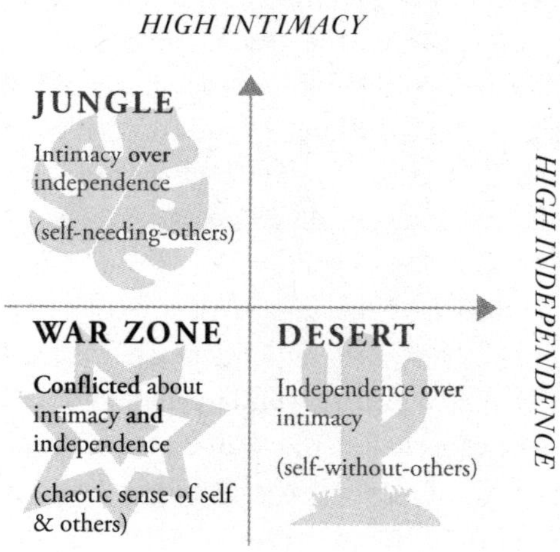

If you're familiar with Internal Family Systems Theory, you probably recognize this language of parts.[6] In essence, each part is employing a strategy to get you what you think you need. That need could be to keep you safe, to make you feel strong, to help you feel good, or to be seen and heard. Each little part is doing its best for you. But each little part is shortsighted. The only strategy it can use is the one it learned in the initial situation with the maturity you had when you experienced it. So if, at four years old, you were beaten for not eating all your food, a part of you might have decided to always eat everything you were given, even if you weren't hungry. Now, as an adult, it feels impossible to stop eating when you're full because your four-year-old attach part is forcing you to keep eating out of fear of punishment and disconnection.

Your attach parts desperately want to connect, to belong, to be with others. Because they are seeking intimacy, these parts learn some of the Jungle survival skills, prioritizing intimacy and proximity. But these parts are also highly fearful and anxious because connection always comes with a cost. You come to expect pleasurable moments will be accompanied by painful ones. Intimate affection is connected to abusive anger. Deep down, you might even start confusing pain and pleasure because relational intimacy was often combined with physical injury or sexual abuse.

These attach parts learn the survival strategies of the Jungle, connecting to and even manipulating social and emotional situations. These parts rejoice in new friendships but might easily feel betrayed. Sometimes these parts will put relationships through manufactured tests of loyalty, insisting that people take sides against others or creating extreme demands on time and schedule. They might change things at the last minute and cut people off if they fail to adjust. These attach parts might give up all boundaries and regularly mistake sexual activity for emotional intimacy, opening you up to being taken advantage of. These parts can easily slip into or create codependent relationships.

Your defend parts, however, want to keep distance and maximize independence. These parts are *counter*dependent. They learn some of the Desert survival skills, using them to fight and flee when needed or to control others (and yourself) through threats and intimidation. Maybe you find yourself regularly bailing out of friendship commitments or abruptly ending romantic relationships. Some defend parts will freeze and shut down, physically disappearing or mentally dissociating. But other defend parts might be adrenaline junkies, using adventure—even danger—as a means for maintaining distance and asserting independence.

Defend parts will fight against admissions of weakness or vulnerability. These parts, using the Desert survival skills, argue that other people are to blame and you can only rely on yourself. These defend parts will often prey on the weaknesses and vulnerabilities of others as a way of protecting themselves. This even happens internally as the defend parts will fight against the attach parts, thinking of them as weak, helpless, and hopeless.[7]

If you grew up in the War Zone, you are probably quite familiar with the feeling of being at war with yourself. Tragically, you probably direct a lot of anger at parts of yourself while cutting other parts of yourself off. Sometimes the defend parts take the lead in your internal war and refuse to interact with the attach parts, which they see as "not-me" or "bad-me." Other times the attach parts might take control by denying or dissociating from the defend parts by lying about or ignoring bad behavior.[8]

These attach and defend parts—at war with each other within the War Zone—are distortions of how God made us for connection and protection, distortions caused by traumatizing relational environments. Our need for connection is expressed through our desire for attaching to others and learning to love and serve them appropriately. Our need for protection is expressed through the appropriate use of fight, flee, freeze, or fawn behaviors in the face of life-threatening situations. But in the War Zone, these God-given instincts toward connection and protection splinter off and disintegrate into parts that attach and defend against themselves and others, all gathered within a body and brain exhausted by chronic anxiety, fear, and loneliness. Ultimately, the War Zone becomes a place where you constantly feel afraid, angry, and ashamed.

And that's not God's good design for you. And it's not the end of your story either. In order to see how you might find peace and joy with God, we need to spend just a little more time on understanding how growing up in the War Zone might impact your faith in God and your experience of church.

Chaotic Faith and the War Zone God

Those raised in the War Zone will have contradictory experiences of God and God's people.

Some will assume that God is just like the War Zone. This War Zone god might be available for care and comfort when help is needed but is also threatening and vindictive, doling out harm to those who deserve it. God is loving, but God is also terrifying and should be respected at all times. Those who see God as a War Zone god might channel their anger toward those who break God's rules while also seeing themselves as blameless in all things (this would be characteristic of a defend part relating to God). Others in the War Zone might be desperate to experience God's love but are convinced by their shame that they are totally unworthy to receive it (this is characteristic of an attach part longing for intimacy but fearing rejection). Others raised in the War Zone might fully identify with God as love. They might be champions of God's love for others, perhaps even aggressively so. But they also might never feel loved and accepted by God themselves.

It's also not uncommon for someone in the War Zone to experience satisfaction when considering the judgment of God. Because they have been the victims of violence, the idea of God judging sinners can be extremely comforting. They might assume that anyone who doesn't completely and fully understand and support them in every situation is automatically going to hell or is at least on the wrong side of truth. When this is the case, they believe that their cause is just and that God backs them up in every conflict. They are innocent, and God will judge the other person.

Others might turn the judgment toward themselves. This is especially true if they hold themselves responsible for their compliance in unspeakable situations as children, even if that compliance was the only option for survival. Others judge themselves for engaging in behaviors or addictions that have blocked God's love and mercy.

War Zone dwellers can be quick to leave churches over what might seem like a small misunderstanding to others. To the War Zone dweller, it's not small at all. This is usually a case of the defend parts overpowering the attach parts. Whatever good work the attach parts have done to find connection in a community is undone by the defend parts, which refuse to work toward reconciliation and would prefer to just leave and start over somewhere else. Others might remain in dysfunctional or even abusive church environments because they blame themselves or don't see themselves as worthy of safety and respect. In their minds, harmful connection is better than no connection at all.

Most churches are not well equipped to accompany people in the War Zone. Without compassionately understanding where some of the erratic attach and defend behaviors are coming from, it can be difficult for people in other landscapes to welcome War Zone individuals into community.

Not Feeling Safe in the Church

If you find yourself living from the War Zone, we empathize with you that there are not a lot of church communities that feel like a soft place to land. We know you've been shunned, villainized, avoided, or ignored. That's not the way God intends church families to work. You've probably also done some of the shunning, villainizing, avoiding, and ignoring. But it's never too late—for you or the church.

Through seeking encounters with Jesus, participating in groups committed to building relational and maturity skills in facilitated communities, engaging in individual counseling, and incorporating secure attachment practices, some War Zone dwellers that I (Cyd) have had the honor of coaching have made incredible progress toward the Pasture. You are not too complicated for Jesus to understand you, and you are not too broken for Jesus to heal. You are meant for the Pasture, just as much as anyone else!

We also invite you to continue with the rest of this book, trying to hold curiosity for both your attach and defend parts. Parts of you will resonate with Jungle descriptions and practices, while other parts will resonate with Desert descriptions and practices. Both can be beneficial for you. Also notice the tension or the inner battle between the impulses to attach and to defend. Trying not to analyze, criticize, or figure yourself out, just acknowledge what you're noticing and offer it to Jesus. He is the one who always understands you even better than you understand yourself. He knows how you got to where you are. He has compassion for you and wants to offer you consistent kindness to lead you out of the War Zone and into the Pasture.

If you're reading this as someone who hasn't experienced the War Zone, the best thing you can do to love your brothers and sisters in the War Zone is to grow your own capacity for joy, keep developing strength in intimacy and independence, and lean into the *yes* defaults. Invite others in your church community to do the same. The more people in your community who can understand where War Zone attachment comes from and who have the capacity to compassionately welcome and weather the unintentional storms of a War Zone dweller, the better the Good News will sound to someone who so desperately wants to find their way home to the Pasture.

The work of healing isn't just limited to the individual who survived the War Zone. Our communities need to become places that can handle the conflict of the attach and defend parts as we all grow together toward the security of the Pasture. Jesus invites all of us! We need to become communities that have the capacity to be as welcoming as Jesus.

Reflection

What ideas about the War Zone were helpful to you in this chapter?

To what extent do you identify with the description of growing up in a War Zone? How did reading this chapter increase your compassion for yourself or for someone you know who might have grown up in the War Zone?

Which of the survival strategies do you see yourself or someone you know using? How have they helped or hindered connections with others, God, or even yourself?

Where do you see the two sides of the War Zone (attach and defend) showing up in your life or in the life of someone you know? How does knowing the two sides increase your understanding or compassion for yourself or your loved one?

If you tried making Jungle and Desert pictures for the previous chapters' reflections, try laying them side by side. What is it like to notice the contrasts? What becomes clearer as you see the differences between the two? Now try putting one on top of the other. Can you see the other picture behind the one on top? Now switch and put the other one on top. Rapidly switch them and notice what happens as you see the Jungle shifting to Desert and back and forth. How do you imagine it must feel to have your internal world shift this quickly?

Try having a conversation with Jesus about what you've resonated with in this chapter.

CHAPTER 8

PASTURE GOD: A CONFIDENT FAITH

Our work in local church ministry, youth ministry, and parenting two sons has put us into contact with quite a few teenagers over the years. In our interactions with young adults making their way into the world for the first time, we have had the joy of celebrating with them when they discovered they had what it took and the honor of processing with them when they ran up against obstacles.

Ethan was home after his first year of college, and we spent some time reconnecting with him. As he talked about his experience of moving to an unfamiliar place, making new friends, finding a new job, learning to pay bills on time, and handling more adult problems, a few things stood out in the way he described his year.

First, Ethan had stayed connected with his parents—not because he needed them but because he valued their wisdom. He called them to celebrate the small wins and asked for their feedback on situations he was facing. He would listen to their input and then make his own decision on how he wanted to handle things. He was leaning into intimacy with his family while also being confident in his ability to take independent action. He knew his family was available to him, but he was okay being away from them.

Second, Ethan had a prevailing sense of hope. Ethan found it difficult to form meaningful connections because his classmates seemed distracted, less than present. Ethan was probably experiencing the difficulty of making connections with people who were living in survival mode as they faced new hurdles away from home. But Ethan could tolerate the distress. He didn't feel the need to try harder. He didn't question his own likability or worth, and he didn't criticize anyone else. Instead, he tried to enjoy the connections he could make at the level people were able to connect. He told us, "I have some great friends here [back home], and I don't mind spending some time alone. I'll keep meeting people, and eventually I'll make some good connections."

Finally, Ethan was able to engage the world beyond him while still remaining himself. He shared how much he was learning about people who were different from him. He had been offered drugs and alcohol and had easily declined them without becoming judgmental or cutting people off. He listened to a new friend share some deep life problems and offered empathy and words of encouragement without feeling responsible for helping him fix anything. Ethan had healthy boundaries, knowing how to care for himself while also being open to the people around him.

Ethan was living in the Pasture.

The Pasture

Imagine you are a sheep in a lush meadow. A sparkling clear stream meanders along the edge, cutting a graceful curve into the sprawling, dense, green carpet of grass. Huge oak trees spread their canopies over the grass, providing pockets of deep, cool shade from the sun. There are places to eat and places to rest.

A strong, attentive shepherd walks among the grazing sheep, humming a tune. As he passes each sheep, he calls it by name and stoops to take a good look at it. He wipes eyes, pulls burrs from wool, and checks hooves. He digs his hands into their thick coats and gives each one an affectionate scratch.

Life in the pasture is peaceful. You have plenty of grass to eat, water to drink, other sheep to interact with, and a caring shepherd who protects you from predators and keeps an eye on your health. When storms come, the shepherd guides you into shelter. When snow covers the grass, he provides hay, barley, and corn that he has stored up for you. Life isn't perfect, but the pasture—and especially the shepherd in it—supplies the refuge and the resources you need to thrive.

Life in the Pasture

Psalm 23 is probably already familiar to you. Artistic depictions of this psalm are everywhere, from coffee mugs to fine art wall hangings. It is read at countless funerals and sick beds and has likely appeared in more Christian books than almost any other passage of Scripture.

This psalm is so appealing because it offers a compelling picture of the way we are designed to live—deeply attached God, the Good Shepherd who leads us to green pastures alongside quiet waters.

David most likely wrote this psalm during his days of keeping sheep, long before he became king of Israel. In this song, David expresses the faith, hope, and love of one who is deeply attached to God. Yes, David had his fair share of mistakes and issues in his adult life, but from reading this psalm, it's also clear that he is writing from a place of secure attachment with God.

In the previous insecure landscapes, the main factor was always who was there for you and how they acted toward you. It is the same with David in the Pasture. He begins by declaring who God is and what God is doing: "The Lord is my shepherd, I lack nothing" (Psalm 23:1). God is available to David as his shepherd. And God is alleviating David's distress so that he can say he has all he needs. The shepherd's sole purpose in being out in the field, sleeping under the stars, and wandering the hillsides is to be available to tend the sheep.

He makes sure the sheep have food, water, and a safe place to sleep. His focus is on the well-being of the sheep.

As the psalm continues, David writes about being in the valley of the shadow of death and eating in the presence of enemies. This sounds like distress. But even in the shadow of death, David does not fear, because the Shepherd is with him. He is not alone. He knows the Shepherd is ready to fend off predators with his rod and pull him back to safety with his staff. And in the presence of enemies, the Shepherd spreads a feast before him. There is no distress that the Shepherd cannot rescue him from. This distress will be alleviated because the Shepherd is available.

Agency might be a little harder to pick up on in Psalm 23, but it's there in the last line: "I will dwell in the house of the LORD forever" (verse 6). We know God won't force us to stay in the place he has designed for us and won't always intervene to keep us out of trouble of our own making. Adam and Eve ignored God's warning and ate of the forbidden tree. Israel refused to follow God's good commandments and lost the Promised Land. The rich young ruler walked away after Jesus invited him to give what he had to the poor and follow Jesus. We have the freedom to ignore, refuse, and waste God's abundant provision and tender care. If we are to dwell in the house of the Lord forever, we must choose to do so. We can use our agency to stay close to God and flourish in the life God has given us.

In all of these ways, David writes from his default *yes* of secure attachment with God. He recognizes the Lord is his Shepherd and he lacks nothing. He dwells in faith, hope, and love. Even though at times throughout his life he will leave the house of the Lord, he always responds to God's invitations to repair the ruptures he has created. He repents and returns to joy each time. He comes back home.

The Green Light of the Pasture

Growing up in the Pasture means having a strong foundation of joyful connection. This foundation of joy grows into a wide window of tolerance that can handle complex emotions and circumstances while still feeling like you—the you God created you to be. Living in the Pasture means being comfortable pursuing intimacy and practicing independence. It means living out of faith, hope, and love and repairing ruptures when they happen.

In the Pasture, you live with a green light. The Jungle flashes a yellow light of *maybe* that prioritizes intimacy. The Desert has a red light of *no* that focuses on independence. And the War Zone has a broken stoplight that causes chaotic movements of intimacy and independence. But in the Pasture, you have a green light that allows you to move forward with care and confidence, pursuing intimacy and practicing independence in a balanced and creative way.

You live from a resounding *yes*.

Yes, someone is available to me. My people are accessible, ready, and willing to be with me.

> *Ethan knew his parents and friends were available to him. He carried his close connections with him as a deep sense of belonging, which gave him the freedom to tolerate some feelings of not yet belonging when he moved away.*

Yes, this distress will be alleviated. Life is not easy and perfectly comfortable, but ruptures are reparable and circumstances change. No pain lasts forever.

> *Ethan could trust that, even if he didn't make friends immediately, he could continue to meet people and lean into new connections. He could also endure challenging circumstances at his new job or in his classes because he knew he could learn and figure things out.*

Yes, I have agency, and I can use it for the good of other people and the good of the world.

> *Living from this default gives Ethan the confidence to navigate the world. He knows that whenever there is a rupture, repair is possible as he figures it out himself or turns to others to help him. And he knows that he has agency to*

be responsible for himself, to take action on his own behalf and on behalf of (and for the sake of) others.

Pasture Thrival Skills

When you live from the Pasture, you have access to all of the survival skills of both the Jungle and the Desert, but you use them not just to survive but to thrive. So instead of being survival skills, they are thrival skills.[1] These skills draw from an integration of intimacy and independence.

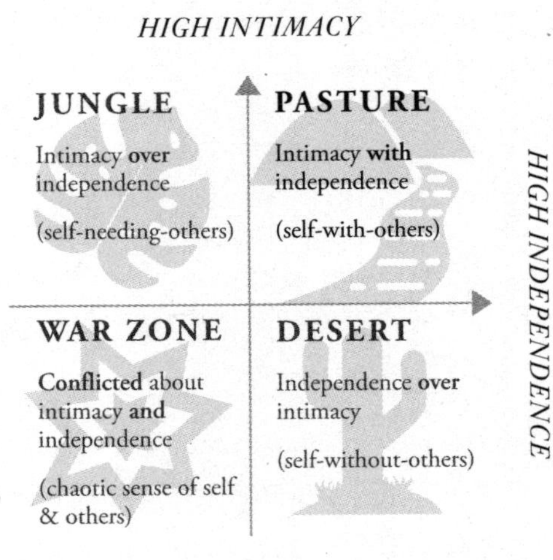

#1. Integrated Processing

Rather than prioritizing social-emotional and nonverbal information (as in the Jungle) or focusing on logical, linear, and verbal communication (as in the Desert), you integrate both processes.[2] You are open and focused on what people are saying with their words, in their emotions, and through their bodies. You are accepting of your feelings and the feelings of others but also know that other facts might need to be considered. In the Pasture, you are neither a "mindless body" knocked around by emotions and instincts nor a "bodiless mind" driven by cognitive clarity and certainty seeking. Rather, you are flexible and adaptable to the emotional and cognitive information in and around you, integrating mind, body, and emotions so you can use all this information to make the best decision. You are able to love God and others with your heart, soul, mind, and strength.

> *During his first month in a new city, Ethan could be honest with himself about feeling lonely, and he didn't shame himself for calling home more than he thought he would (social-emotional processing). He also reminded himself that it takes time to make new friends, so this wasn't a problem that needed to be solved right away. It was more like a situation he needed to live through (cognitive-logical processing). While it felt bad, he knew it wasn't a crisis.*

#2. Accountable Relationships

Rather than disregarding rules for the sake of relationships or compromising relationships for the sake of rules, a securely attached person knows that close relationships are fostered by clear rules. Thriving relationships have and respect boundaries, hold each other accountable to expectations, and hold shared values and standards. Rules are not adopted and enforced in an authoritarian manner, where one person dominates the rest. Nor are rules carelessly cast aside in a permissive way, where one person carries the burden of the relationship while others skip out on their responsibilities.[3] In the Pasture, holding all relationships accountable is a thrival skill practiced in community.

> *Ethan developed a friendship with Logan, who struggled with anxiety. While Ethan was willing to listen to Logan's worries and concerns and offer him reassurance, he also needed Logan to ask him how he was doing. Ethan had a conversation with Logan about this. He shared his support and concern for Logan while also expressing his own needs for a reciprocal friendship.*

#3. Emotional Regulation

In the Jungle, you "go to your people" to help you *coregulate* when you are distressed and emotionally dysregulated because you don't feel you can solve your problems on your own. In the Desert, you "do it yourself" as a means of *solo-regulation* when distressed because you don't trust others to help you solve your problems. These are lopsided survival skills.

But in the Pasture, you develop the thrival skill of emotional regulation. This means you can choose between emotional coregulation (with others) and solo-regulation (alone). You are flexible enough to use either strategy.[4] You neither need people to solve your problems nor need to solve them yourself. People are neither the problem nor the solution but are available to partner with you in solving the problem if needed. You are capable of doing things yourself (practicing independence), but you are also capable of asking others for help (pursuing intimacy).

At one point during his school year, Ethan experienced tooth pain for a few days and took ibuprofen, did some deep breathing, and flossed extra to see if that would resolve it. Finally, the pain was too extreme. He knew he needed help. He called his mom and admitted he was scared and in a lot of pain. She gave him the emergency number for his home dentist and asked if he wanted to call for himself or would prefer that she call. After talking with her, crying a little, and calming down, he decided he could call.

#4. Mutually Owning Faults

The last thrival skill is specifically concerned with rupture and repair. While Jungle, Desert, and War Zone dwellers often focus on who's to blame for ruptures, living in the Pasture is all about seeking repair. It's not all your fault. It's not all their fault. Everyone plays a part in relational ruptures, so we all need to be skilled at mutually owning our faults. You don't need to defensively ignore or deny the role you play in a rupture. And you don't need to defend or ignore the role someone else played. Using your integrated processing (thrival skill #1) while holding relationships accountable (thrival skill #2) and staying within your window of tolerance through self-regulation (thrival skill #3) means everyone can own their faults without feeling like their vulnerability will be taken advantage of.

While Ethan was away at school, he was also planning his brother's bachelor party. Ethan is not always great at returning text messages, and so both his brother and some of the groomsmen felt frustrated about the lack of clarity around what was happening. Ethan's brother confronted him about it. Ethan was initially defensive but then recognized he didn't need to protect himself from his brother. He recognized that, while prioritizing his schoolwork, he had not been clearly communicating about the bachelor party, which he had already planned. He also apologized to the groomsmen while expressing some frustration that too many people were trying to get involved in the planning. His brother recognized that he was making assumptions about lack of planning, and the groomsmen recognized they had jumped in, thinking Ethan didn't have it covered. Everyone owned their part and returned to joy. Ethan clarified communication, and when the bachelor party was over, everyone agreed he had done a great job planning it.

Invitation into the Pasture

As you've read this description of secure attachment and life in the Pasture, you may be celebrating your secure attachment and your wide range of thrival skills. But it's likely that you are feeling discouraged. Maybe the Pasture feels so far away that you can't imagine finding yourself there. In reality, no one ever lives continually from these thrival skills. We fall into protection mode and live from our lopsided survival skills of the Jungle, Desert, or War Zone. Ruptures will happen. The point isn't to never experience ruptures or never fall into your old attachment strategies. The point is to recognize you've left the Pasture, make repairs, and return.

No matter where you find yourself, let these words sink in: You *can* move deeper into the Pasture. You *can* accept the invitation of the Good Shepherd to follow him into greater security in your attachment with him and with other people.

We know this because the Good Shepherd was not content just to be talked about or read about in Psalm 23. Rather, the Good Shepherd took on flesh and dwelled among us, coming to find his lost sheep, laying down his life so that they might live (see John 1:14; 10:11; Luke 15:4). This Good Shepherd is Jesus—God with us.

Jesus, our Good Shepherd, is leading us into the Pasture where our attachment defaults shift to *yes*.

Yes—in Jesus, God is available to you. You can always talk to him in prayer, and he cares what you have to say. You can trust Jesus to meet you where you are.

Yes—in Jesus, this distress will be alleviated. God is with you, even in the hardest of places, and his companionship gives you hope that this won't last forever. Even when circumstances in this world feel impossible, you know that this life is not the end of the story. God is always doing something, and he is not finished yet.

Yes—in Jesus, you have agency. You can choose to follow the Good Shepherd, and you can choose to obey the good guidelines God has given. You can bless others with the same blessing you have received from God, and you can love with the same love you have received.

This is how Jesus repairs our attachment ruptures. This is how we become deeply attached to God.

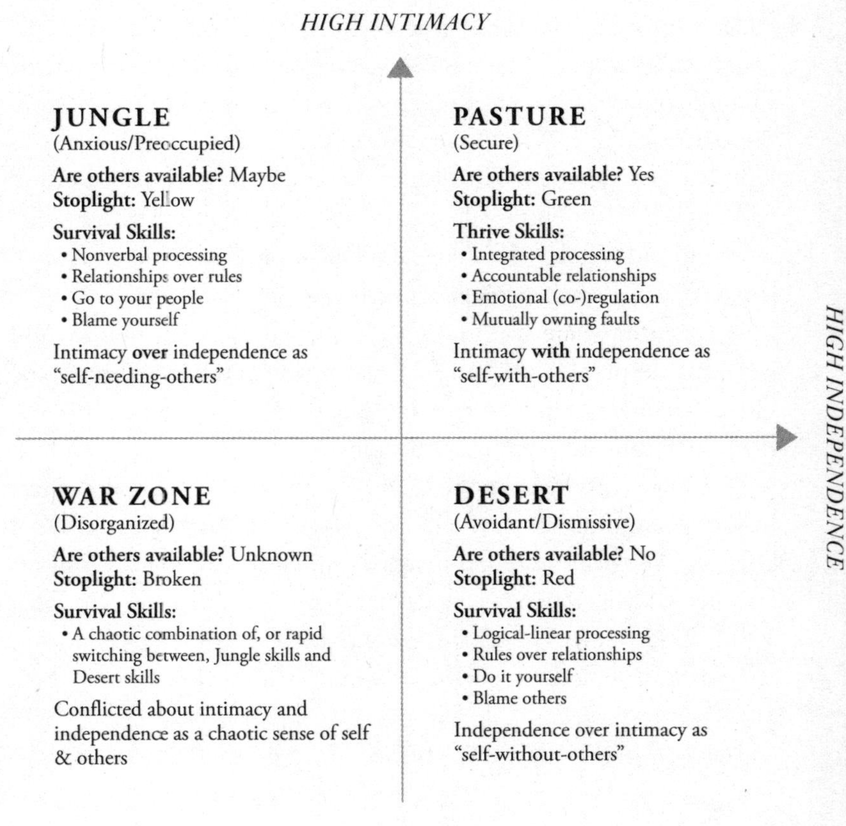

Reflection

What sounds like good news to you in this chapter?

What about the Pasture is especially attractive to you?

What thrival skills do you see showing up in your life or in the life of someone you know?

Try drawing the Pasture. What feels inviting to you about the Pasture?

How do you think it would feel to live from the Pasture? What would be different about your posture toward the world? Toward other people? Yourself? God?

Try having a conversation with Jesus about what you've resonated with in this chapter.

INTERLUDE

MOVING FROM WHERE YOU ARE

Imagine a large table. Half the table looks and feels solid. The other half is made of clear plexiglass, creating the appearance of a visual cliff or sudden drop. A nine-month-old baby is placed on the solid side, unaware of the change in the middle of the table. The mother is on the far side of the table. Then the mother reveals a favorite toy and coaxes the baby over to her. So the baby starts crawling across the table. But when the plexiglass cliff appears, the baby stops, afraid of falling. Uncertainty and fear are building. What is she going to do? In the face of danger or uncertainty, a baby automatically looks to the face of their attachment figure.

This is when the experiment really starts.

Researchers trained each mom to give their baby a different facial expression right as the baby looked up when they got to the visual cliff. Using only their faces (not voice or body), the moms expressed joy, interest, fear, or anger. The researchers wanted to see what the babies would do when they saw different emotions from their mothers. The experiment found that babies would venture into the unknown—crawling onto an invisible table—when they saw joy and interest on their mother's face. But the babies backed away from the cliff when they saw fear or anger.

Looking at the face of your attachment figure to receive nonverbal information about the environment is called *social referencing*.[1] This is how children learn to evaluate what is going on around them, whether things are safe to approach or should be avoided. By referencing the face of our attachment figure, we learn if we should start or stop a behavior, what is right and wrong, and what is good and bad. This nonverbal process is how we internalize the emotions and values of our attachment figures and, by extension, our community.

As we seek to leave the solid wood of our familiar attachment strategies and move into the unknown territory of the Pasture, we must look to the face of Jesus, our Good Shepherd. As we share social referencing with Jesus and with others who are attaching to Jesus, we can begin to discern when we are heading toward faith, hope, and love and when we are heading off a cliff.

Where We've Been and Moving Forward

We've explored God's good design for us to live in secure attachment (part 1). We've looked at how being deeply attached comes from the *one desire* for joyful connection, the *two dimensions* of intimacy and independence, growing into the *three* attachment defaults. This is the compelling vision for life that motivates us toward spiritual and relational transformation. Then we visited the Jungle of Anxiety, the Desert of Avoidance, and the War Zone of Chaos and described how our distorted defaults come to be and the lopsided survival skills we develop to cope (part 2). Now it's time to move into the opportunity to leave where we find ourselves and follow Jesus deeper into the Pasture.

But before we do, let's acknowledge that you might have emerged from the last three chapters feeling confused. Maybe you find yourself identifying with more than one of the landscapes. Maybe you're investigating your childhood and having trouble making sense of how you ended up using the strategies you're using. You might be trying to figure it all out and explain how you arrived in the landscape you're living from.

It's common to identify with parts of the Jungle and parts of the Desert. That doesn't mean you're automatically located in a War Zone. As we mentioned, you were amazingly good at adapting to your environment when you were young. If you grew up in more than one home or had extremely different caregivers, it's entirely possible that you learned to switch between landscapes, depending on who you were with. It's also possible that, by this point in your life, you have worked hard to gain skills you knew you needed but didn't have from your childhood.[2]

Homing In on Your Current Location

In order to home in on your most current and most dominant attachment landscape, think of the person you are currently most attached to in your life. That could be a parent, a spouse, a grandparent, a boyfriend or girlfriend, or a best friend. This is the person who is there for you.

Now, imagine being in conflict with that person. How do you respond? Do you respond in a Jungle way, blaming yourself, seeking a quick resolution, or going to other trusted people to help you figure it out? Or do you respond in a Desert way, blaming the other person, being indifferent to reconciliation, and just waiting things out until everything returns to normal?

Noticing which landscape you are in is part of the process of moving toward the Pasture. But it's less important to explain exactly where you are or how you arrived here. You might not remember all the relational and emotional learning you did in intense moments of your early life. You don't actually need to. Rather than reliving all your traumas, it's more important to recognize that you likely have a very good reason for picking up the strategies you did. You were trying to survive. Without these strategies, you wouldn't be where you are today.

But you probably picked up this book because you're not completely content with where you are. You can recognize that you're likely not living from the Pasture of secure attachment. Not all of your survival strategies are still serving you. Many are outdated, no longer necessary. And they are especially not necessary in your relationship with God. But you likely use them with God just as you do with people.

Our goal in writing this book is to help you compassionately recognize which survival strategies you've imported into your relationship with God and to focus on shifting into a more secure attachment with God.

The good news is that Jesus, our Good Shepherd, wants to lead you from where you find yourself in the Jungle, Desert, or War Zone into the Pasture. Jesus offers you a deeply attached life that goes beyond mere survival.

Meeting and Moving

Jesus meets you right where you are. In whatever landscape you find yourself, Jesus comes to you right there.

Just as Jesus ate with sinners and tax collectors, touched the unclean, mingled with Gentiles, and spoke to women in socially unacceptable ways, Jesus is willing to meet with you in whatever condition or location you find yourself. You are not beyond his availability. He is glad to meet with you—anywhere, anytime.

In fact, Jesus already meets with you. If you're reading this book, you must already feel some desire for a deeper connection with God. It is evidence of God's goodness and mercy that, in some ways, he meets us on our own terms. The ways we first become aware of God's presence in our life are often familiar attachment pathways for us. Jesus knows what we need in order to recognize him as an attachment possibility—even if that means meeting us in a way that fits with our current insecurities and attachment strategies.

But Jesus doesn't just meet us in our insecure survival strategies. He also moves us toward a deeper and fuller life. He meets us in our surviving and moves us toward thriving.[3]

When Jesus sees us surviving in our ruptured worlds, he longs to repair all that is bent and confused and bring us to a life of thriving. He wants to replace our survival skills with thrival skills. He wants to rebuild our foundation of joyful connection, strengthen our capacities for intimacy and independence, and rewrite our defaults to a wholehearted yes. Jesus doesn't just meet us where we are. Jesus also invites us to follow him to even greener pastures, even cleaner waters. He longs for us to truly dwell in the house of the Lord. And for that to happen, we have to move from where we are.

In order for Jesus to bring us deeper into the Pasture, he needs to go beyond meeting us and begin moving us. As our Good Shepherd, Jesus won't leave us in the same patch of green grass for our entire lives. Nibbling from the same patch without moving would produce fat and lazy sheep with sluggish hearts and weak bodies. Just as the psalmist passes through the valley of the shadow of death in order to dwell in the house of the Lord forever, Jesus moves us beyond the easier encounters where he first meets us into territory that challenges us to release our insecure attachments and become stronger in our attachment with him.

Jesus meets us right where we are *and* he invites us to move further and deeper into the Pasture by learning new skills to deepen our secure attachment.

How to Read Part 3: Moving from Where You Are

As you read the coming chapters about how Jesus, our Good Shepherd, invites us into his securely attached life with the Father and the Spirit, some of those invitations will feel easier for you than others. Some aspects of Jesus' life will feel like Jesus *meeting* you. Jesus meets you in your insecurity through the survival skills you already have. Other parts of Jesus' life will feel like he is *moving* you. In order to follow Jesus into this part of his securely attached life, you will need to make a move or ask him to move you.

In other words, some aspects of Jesus' life will feel comfortable (meeting), and some will be challenging (moving), depending on which landscape you're starting from. We want to encourage you to celebrate and enjoy being met by Jesus while also stretching yourself to stay open to Jesus moving you.

In order to change your defaults, you need to try new experiments with Jesus as your attachment figure. When you gather new data, you can draw new conclusions that can start to shift your defaults. It won't be easy, and it might not happen very quickly. It took your whole life to get where you are; it will take a little while to move on. But the good news is that all of us are invited to follow our Good Shepherd further and deeper into the Pasture. All of us are invited to become more deeply attached to God.

PART 3

GOD'S REPAIR: DEEPLY ATTACHED

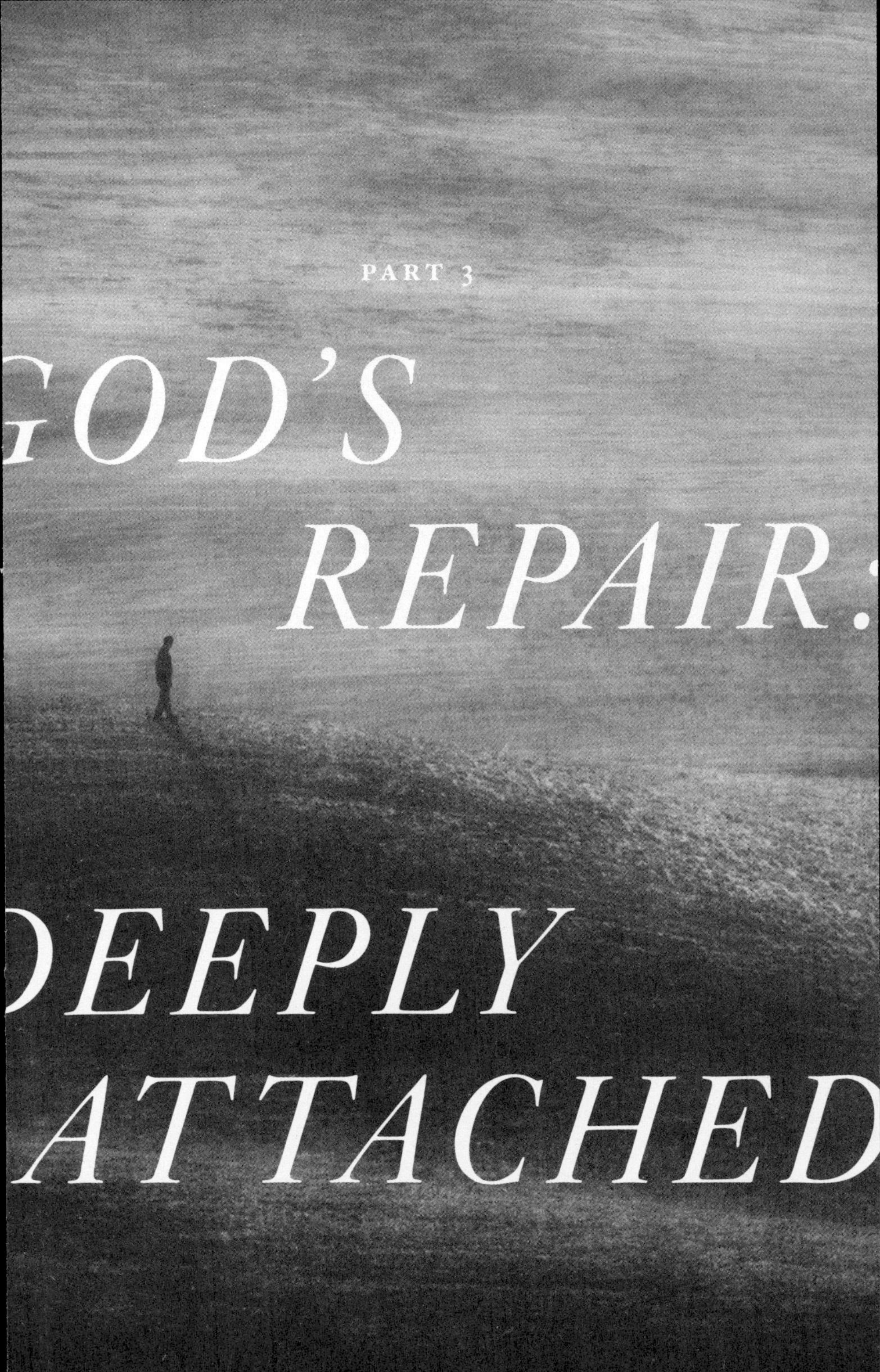

CHAPTER 9

BAPTIZED WITH JESUS: ENCOUNTERING JOY

We started this book looking at the *good roots* of attachment as God designed it, examining our early development: the one foundational desire for joyful connection, how this foundation grows into the two interrelated dimensions of intimacy and independence, and how this all gets internalized as the three defaults of faith, hope, and love. Then we looked at how things have *gone wrong* because of sin and how we develop distorted attachments and ruptured relationships. Now we move into *God's repair* of these ruptures and how this happens in and through Jesus.

This repair of our attachment ruptures must happen at two different levels: human and divine.

On the human level, we need help. Our everyday lives are full of ups and downs, joys and pains, triumphs and traumas. Just like kids, we are still gathering data from our attachment experiments on a daily basis. To repair our attachment with God, there are things we need to practice every day so we can collect new data in our attachment history with God.

But this repair also needs to reach the deepest parts of us, the spiritual depths (and heights) of life with God. Attachment needs to reach our souls. But we can't make that happen. Kids can't reach up and make attachment happen with their parents. Instead, the parents have to offer attachment to their children. In the same way, we can't make our attachment with God happen. God has to reach down and offer the gift of attachment to us. We receive it by God's grace, as the gift of love. This is the divine level of attachment.

So, for this last part of the book, when we talk about Jesus, we will be moving between two levels. On the human level, Jesus *models* a secure attachment with God. Jesus shows us what it looks like to live as one who is deeply attached to his Father. This is the fully human Jesus.

But on the divine level, Jesus offers us the gift of attachment with him. Jesus offers everything an attuned parent offers. Jesus *meets* us in our insecure survival strategies and helps *move* us toward secure attachment. To follow Jesus is to become attached to him, and to become attached to Jesus is to become attached to God. This is the fully divine Jesus.

In Jesus, God is available to us to alleviate our distress and activate our agency. We become deeply attached to God by practicing our attachment to Jesus, our Good Shepherd, who leads us out of our anxious Jungles, avoidant Deserts, and chaotic War Zones into the Pasture of Joy and Peace.

So let's see how Jesus repairs our ruptures.

Encountering Jesus (Immanuel Prayer)

At the end of the Gospel of Matthew, Jesus tells his disciples that he will be with them until the end of the age (see Matthew 28:20). If Jesus is always with us, then it stands to reason that he is with us in our ordinary moments, even though we are not usually looking for him.

Immanuel prayer is a practice that takes these words seriously, assuming the presence of God with us in the moment. In Immanuel prayer, we help each other become joyfully connected to God, knowing that God is always glad to be with us.[1]

I (Cyd) have facilitated Immanuel prayer experiences for people for almost fifteen years. Whenever I pray with them, I start by having them recall a strong memory of joy. They can choose a time when they felt connected with God, or they might choose a time when they were connected with a friend, a family member, or even a pet. If they don't remember experiencing gladness to be with someone, I might ask them to remember a time when they felt everything was good and right in the world, a time when they felt safe and calm, at peace.

I ask them to describe the experience as fully as they can. To go back to the memory and walk around in it. To describe what they're seeing, hearing, feeling, smelling, tasting. Brain scans show that when we recall a memory, our brain experiences it as if it's happening now. And so, by recalling a memory of a time when they experienced joy, they experience that joy all over again, in an embodied way. They are practicing connection in their nervous system and strengthening their foundation of joy.

Once that memory is fresh, I will ask them to invite Jesus to be with them there. And then, together, they become curious about how Jesus might be present in this memory. If Jesus is truly with us all the time, he must be here. How would Jesus like them to know he's here? Sometimes people will see Jesus immediately. Other times, they might feel a warmth or a weight, see a light, or just sense his company. Whether a person can experience the presence of Jesus or not, together we just keep remembering the joyful memory and even remember other times of joy. The joy is so good for our brains that even if that's all they do, it's still healing in its own way.

If they begin to notice and experience Jesus with them, I will often encourage them to ask, "What do you have for me today?"

More often than not, Jesus seems to have a simple agenda. Almost always, he invites people to rest, to be with him. In Immanuel prayer, the two most common things Jesus says to people are some version of "I'm here" and "I love you." Jesus seems to be incredibly focused on rebuilding the foundation of joyful connection in our ordinary lives. After all, Jesus knows how important it is to live from joy. He also lived a human life.

The Everyday Human Life of Jesus

Jesus lived the daily, ordinary life of a Jewish man for about thirty years. We can assume from what we know in Scripture that he regularly went to the synagogue to worship, practiced the Sabbath with his family, and celebrated the festivals of his people.

But there was something very different about Jesus. His joyful foundation with the heavenly Father was different from anyone else's understanding of God. Jesus trusted that he was always welcome in the presence of his Father and that in the Father's presence there was joy.

Most of the Jews in Jesus' day did not feel the same way.

The Pharisees didn't seem to enter the presence of God with much joy. Instead, they were rigid in their practice of faith, seeming to rely more on themselves than on the work of God. They seemed to live from a Desert landscape, using logical-linear tools to learn and create the rules and follow them closely. They blamed Israel's troubles on the sinfulness of others and worked hard to maintain their distance from those not seeking God's holiness in the same way.

The Sadducees seemed more concerned about social, political, and relational dynamics than they were with the joy of God. They seemed to live from a Jungle landscape, watching the shifting landscapes of the political powers and managing relationships with the people who could benefit them most. They prioritized relationships with the Romans over the rules of the Pharisees and kept a close watch on which relationships provided the best opportunities for advancement.

And then there were the Zealots. Living from the War Zone, they adopted a survival stance, prone to violence and lashing out because of the ways the Jews had been oppressed throughout history. They were tired of being the victims and were ready to take matters into their own hands.

Some of these approaches might sound familiar to you as you think of churches you know or stories you hear in the news. God's people have been living from Jungles, Deserts, and War Zones from the beginning. These are fully human survival strategies to cope with the pain of distorted attachments and ruptured relationships.

But Jesus was able to live so differently. How did he resist turning to these survival strategies? Where did his security come from when he was living an ordinary human life within a sinful world?

Jesus' baptism provides some insight.

The Baptism of Jesus

When Jesus is baptized, he comes up out of the water and the Holy Spirit rests on him in bodily form, like a dove. The heavens open, and the Father speaks, "You are my dearly loved Son, and you bring me great joy" (Luke 3:22, NLT).

Because Jesus is not only fully God but also fully human, he has the same need and desire for joyful connection that we all do. His humanity means he is designed for joyful connection as the foundation of his identity.

And in this baptismal moment, the Father and Holy Spirit are reminding Jesus of that joyful connection. God is with him in his earthly life and glad to be with him. This is a moment of returning to joyful connection. The Father and Spirit are communicating delight and availability to Jesus. God is saying, "I am here. I am glad to be with you. I love you." In his full humanity, Jesus is modeling for us how to receive the attachment gift that is offered by his Father.

Remember the blessing God gave to Aaron when the Israelites were an infant people? God is refreshing this blessing with Jesus. The Father's face is shining on Jesus, speaking words of delight over him, putting his name on him, just as he did with Israel (see Numbers 6:27). Jesus is being reminded, in no uncertain terms, who he really is. He is the beloved Son. He is being reminded of the *yes* that he lives from: Yes, the Father and the Spirit are available to him. Joyful connection is his firm foundation. In his humanity, Jesus models being deeply attached to God.

But Jesus doesn't just *show* us the way to deepen our attachment. He *is* the way. In his full divinity, Jesus becomes our attachment figure, offering us deep attachment. "I am the way, the truth, and the life. No one can come to the Father except through me" (John 14:6, NLT).

Jesus Offers Joyful Connection as our Attachment Figure

Everything Jesus models in his baptism he offers us in his divinity. Jesus is the Good Shepherd, and he offers himself as our attachment figure. In Immanuel prayer encounters, he most often says to people, "I'm here" and "I love you." In this way, he offers his presence to us just as the Spirit descended upon him at his baptism. And he expresses affection for us, just as his Father expressed affection for him in the words spoken over him. Jesus, fully divine, is with us in our everyday moments, offering us deep attachment in our ordinary, human lives.

It can sound trite if someone tells you "God is with you" or "Jesus loves you." But it's an entirely different experience to hear Jesus himself say, "I'm here with you" and "I love you."

It's one thing to remember with your cognitive and rational mind that Jesus is present and loves you. You can read it in Scripture and remind yourself of it. And this is important! It's also an entirely different thing to remember a time of joy, *experience* Jesus present with you in it, and then hear him say, "I love you." To experience something like this is to step into the experience of Jesus' baptism with him.

Remember how quickly relational and emotional learning happens compared to rational, cognitive learning? (See chapter 1.) These kinds of encounters with Jesus, where he is with you and says, "I love you" or where the Father says, "You are my beloved," affect us in a way that rehearsing the truth doesn't. Our brains experience these kinds of moments differently. They sink into our implicit memories in a way that takes much longer when we learn them explicitly.[2] And the most incredible news is that the attachment gift that the Father and the Spirit give to Jesus in his baptism is not reserved only for Jesus. It's actually a moment we can all participate in. In Jesus, we are all dearly loved children, bringing joy to the Trinity (see Galatians 4:4-7; Luke 15).

Every single one of us is invited to return to joy and to amplify joy with the Trinity in this baptismal moment. We are all invited to be baptized with Jesus. Each of us can receive Jesus' presence and his delighted affection.

And his invitation into joyful connection can rewrite our attachment histories.

Jesus Restores Our Joyful Connection

About twenty years ago, when I (Cyd) was receiving Immanuel prayer, I asked Jesus, "What do you have for me today?" A memory flashed into my mind, and I asked Jesus if he wanted to lead me there. I sensed his response as an invitation to follow.

It was a memory that my family recalled (to laughter) quite often. Objectively, it *is* funny. But from my point of view, it was also somewhat traumatic. I was about four years old, and my mom had been dating the man who would become my dad. It was a big night because my mom had told us that he would be taking us out for dinner. We got to dress up in fancy clothes, and she wanted us to behave well.

I did my best all night. By the time we got home, I had to go to the bathroom pretty badly . . . so badly that I didn't make it to the bathroom. Instead, I stopped over a heating vent and relieved myself right there, in the living room. Through my red tights.

I remember feeling instantly better. My physical distress had been alleviated. But then I saw the looks of disgust and horror on my mom's, sister's, and future father's faces. I can't blame them for their reactions. It must have been pretty startling. It's not an everyday thing to do, and I can only guess at my mom's horror at imagining the smell the next time the heat kicked on. My sister was probably embarrassed to be related to me, and my future father was probably wondering what in the world he might be getting himself into!

I experienced the moment as utter humiliation. Full-body shame. Any words that came out of their mouths sounded full of venom and fury. I felt despicable and repulsive. It was a full-blown relational rupture.

Looking back on this moment as an adult and knowing what I know about relational neuroscience, I can accurately say that everyone's nervous systems kicked into protection mode. No one was thinking about connection. No one was thinking about how I might experience this as a four-year-old or how I might implicitly carry this memory in my body for the rest of my life. No one could know what it would be like for me to hear this story rehearsed over and over as I grew up. "Remember the time when . . ." was the beginning of a hilarious story for everyone except me. For me, it was a reminder that I was despicable and repulsive. They couldn't know what this story had done to my little nervous system.

In this memory, no one was available to me in my distress. Nobody meant to hurt me, but I internalized this as *No one is glad to be with me.*

When Jesus brought this memory back to me in Immanuel prayer, he brought it to me differently. He was with me in it. I wasn't isolated and afraid, ashamed and humiliated, alone and misunderstood. Instead, Jesus was with me. Right in front of me. Smiling at me.

Jesus was available to me, glad to be with me.

And as he stood with me, looking upon me with kindness, he said, "What a clever choice." And he chuckled—not in a way that made me feel ashamed, but in a way that made me feel smart. He was affirming my agency. In my four-year-old mind, I knew going on the carpet was a bad idea. It made so much more sense to go in what looked remarkably like a drain. Of course, my family thought it was ridiculous to make that choice, but Jesus was honoring it. He knew it made sense to my four-year-old mind.

And this made all the difference. By showing me he was with me and by affirming my agency, Jesus restoried this memory for me. He took this memory of being despicable and repulsive and turned it into an understanding of my creativity and resourcefulness. I was doing the best a four-year-old could do in an impossible situation. And because it was social and emotional learning in a fully embodied way, this new memory with Jesus rewrote the countless times this story had been told throughout my life.

What God graciously healed in me in that Immanuel prayer experience has been affirmed by trauma researchers, attachment researchers, and brain scientists alike. When someone is with us, glad to be with us, we experience everything differently than we do when we're alone.[3] When we are with a compassionate witness, we have a connection that makes us more resilient and able to endure distress and difficult circumstances. When we are alone or disconnected from the people who share the experience with us, it can become traumatic because we don't have the capacity to process or make sense of the experience.

As a four-year-old, I couldn't process all my family members' big emotions. I couldn't have compassion for them and their responses. I didn't have what I needed to make sense of that experience and their reactions to my behavior. And so it turned into a painful memory for me. No one in my family intended to hurt me. No one expected me to carry it for years. But it got stored as pain because no one was able to help me make sense of it.

When Jesus showed me how he was with me in that memory, however, it was no longer a secret shame. It was now shared. It was seen, known, understood. By showing up with compassion and tenderness, Jesus told me, "I'm here with you." And with his affirmation of my clever choice and his affectionate chuckle, he told me, "I love you."

And when Jesus was there with me, I had the capacity to see the memory for what it was. I was able to have compassion for myself, my mom, my sister, and my future father. We all blew it. We all flipped into protection mode, and we all lost our connections to one another. But Jesus didn't. Jesus was available to all of us—even though I couldn't see him in the moment. Connecting with him like this in hindsight forever changed the way that memory is stored in my implicit memory.

And that's just one of countless stories I could tell you about the difference the presence of God makes in our memories. I have had the privilege to facilitate hundreds of Immanuel prayer encounters through the years, and I never grow tired of witnessing what happens when Jesus shows people that he is here. Sometimes he says the words, "I'm here" and "I love you." Other times, he just silently makes himself known and demonstrates his affection. But his presence changes everything.

Returning to Joy In and Through Jesus

You may have never experienced anything like this kind of encounter with Jesus. That's okay. That doesn't mean you can't still return to the joyful connection God intends for you. Even just opening yourself up to the possibility that Jesus is always glad to be with you is a big step into shoring up your foundation of joyful connection.

In this world, we will always have experiences that are beyond our capacity. We will get pushed outside our window of tolerance and flip into protection mode. Not only do we regularly get dysregulated, but the people around us do too. But we are never alone. Jesus is always glad to be with us, and like an attuned parent, he meets us right where we are. He says, "I'm here." Jesus always understands our experience, and his "I love you" gives us his capacity to move into compassion for ourselves and for the people in our lives.

When we find ourselves dysregulated and feeling ashamed, alone, angry, confused, sad, or any other emotion, we can allow Jesus to attune to us—just as God did to Hagar when she ran from Abraham and Sarah. Jesus attunes to us in our distress. We are not alone. We can return to his gladness to be with us. His presence changes everything.

Every time we return to joy with Jesus, we grow our capacity for joyful connection. Growing our capacity for joyful connection increases our capacity for all of life. The primary way we move from wherever we find ourselves toward the Pasture is to rebuild our foundation of joyful connection with God and with other people.

Because that joyful connection is so central to our identity, we need it in order to know who we are. Rebuilding our joyful connection is like coming home. Returning to the joy we are designed for is the invitation Jesus extends to each of us. It's an invitation to return to the joy that Jesus is always glad to be with us.

But depending on which landscape you find yourself in as you read this, you might struggle to receive this part of Jesus' securely attached life as your own.

Jesus Meets You in the Jungle

If you are coming from the Jungle, you may find this whole chapter incredibly inviting. Reading about how Jesus is always glad to be with you and expresses love and affection for you is music to your relational ears. After all, you tend to seek out intimacy and orient your actions around creating and preserving relationships. Jesus *meets* you in those survival strategies by offering deeply personal and intimate ways of relating with you. Enjoy Jesus meeting you in your longing for nonverbal experiences and intimate encounters.

- You can rely on your nonverbal processing strength and use your imagination to allow Jesus to encounter you in your ordinary daily life and in your memories.

- You can prioritize relationship more than rules and find Jesus meeting you in relationship, even when you haven't followed the rules.
- You can find validation in naming your relationally intimate experiences with Jesus as important ways to build your foundation for joyful connection.
- You naturally think of yourself as a self-needing-others, and so when you're in distress, it's more natural for you to want to return to joy with Jesus.
- You appreciate intimacy, and so it might be easier for you to rest in joy-amplifying moments with Jesus rather than rushing through them.

Jesus Moves You Toward the Pasture

Because you are hypervigilant about relationships and always looking for signs of readiness to connect, you might struggle to trust your joyful connection with Jesus when you aren't experiencing anything. If you worship, pray, or journal and it feels dry or empty, you might think you've done something wrong or Jesus has changed his mind about you. You might try to figure out what might have gone wrong or feel pressure to do something different so you experience joy again. Jesus wants to move you from this place of insecure hypervigilance into a stronger trust in his consistency.

As far as we know, Jesus only experienced this baptism kind of encounter once during his earthly life (twice if you count the transfiguration). The rest of the time, Jesus may have been using his cognitive tools to trust the joyful connection with the Father. Here are some tools that you might borrow from your Desert friends to balance to your usual skills:

- Read the Psalms. Many of them are psalms of lament, where the writer cries out to God in distress, wondering where he is. Allow yourself to enter into the experience of what feels like silence from God. You're not the only one who has ever felt this way.

- Recall times of joy and connection with Jesus and allow yourself to experience them again. This is a way of returning to joy when you find yourself in distress or discouragement or even when you're feeling distant. If you haven't already journaled about times when you've felt close with Jesus or experienced his gladness to be with you, write them out. Rereading them is a powerful way to keep building your capacity to return to joyful connection.
- Talk to Jesus about the distance you feel. Be honest with him if you feel more desperate for an experience than you are for a relationship. Ask him to help you trust his closeness, even when you don't feel it.

Jesus Meets You in the Desert

If you find yourself in the Desert, you might have an immediate resistance to this subjective experience of Jesus stuff. For you, this part of Jesus' securely attached life might require movement. But Jesus also meets you here.

You can use your logical-linear tools to make the connections:

- In Jesus, we are all children of God. You likely know all the verses that say this. But if not, read Galatians 4:1-7 and Romans 8:1-17. The logic goes like this: All who live *in* Jesus are children of God. All the children of God receive the same benefits and realities as Jesus. One of the benefits and realities of Jesus was this baptism affirmation and joyful connection. Therefore, if you are in Jesus, you also stand in the waters of baptism with him, receive the attachment the Father offers, and are verified by the Spirit. In your humanity, you can receive the same attachment that Jesus received in his humanity.

- Jesus promises the disciples he will be with them always, to the end of the age (see Matthew 28:20). You are a disciple of Jesus, and it's not yet the end. Therefore, Jesus must still be with you somehow. In his divinity, Jesus offers himself to you as an attachment figure. (We will look more at this in the next chapter.)

Jesus Moves You Toward the Pasture

Because you probably haven't given a lot of priority to cultivating emotion (you weren't given that survival skill), you likely don't allow yourself to sit and savor the reality that God delights in you. Because you've grown accustomed to doing things on your own, assuming no one is available and you must take care of yourself, it's likely extremely challenging for you to open yourself to this kind of joy and delight expressed over you. After all, you haven't done enough to deserve this kind of praise, and you certainly don't see any value in empty affirmation.

But for you, the work is to simply receive. Long before you might ever hear the words "Well done, good and faithful servant," these words at Jesus' baptism are already true. *You are my son, my daughter, in whom I delight.* This is your starting place, whether you can receive it or not.

Allow yourself to be challenged to receive the delight of the Father. Allow yourself to be led by the Good Shepherd into this joy-amplifying moment, receiving the shining face of the Father and the resting presence of the Spirit. You need this. You may not think you do, but you do.

We're All Born into a New Family

When we are baptized, we are adopted into a new family.[4]

Because we are in Christ, we now live Jesus' life with him. This means we share his attachment relationships with the Father and the Spirit.

Jesus returns to joy in the "I'm here" and amplifies joy in the "I love you" of his baptism. As your Good Shepherd, he invites you to join him in the waters of the Jordan River. The words spoken over Jesus and all the meaning they carry are not just for Jesus. These words are for you. And they are words you can live by.

A Practice for All Landscapes: Examen of Joyful Connection

For the next several chapters, we encourage you to build a practice of **Examen**, *or a simple practice of reflecting on your day with Jesus.*

- *Begin by taking a couple of deep breaths—in through your nose and out through your mouth. As you do this, remember God's gladness to be with you, no matter how you come into this time. Ask the Holy Spirit to help you notice what you need to notice.*
- *Begin by recalling your day in the order in which it happened, with an eye toward finding the good things.*
- *Now thank God for these things. Appreciate them as specific gifts, expressions of God's care for you.*
- *Now review the day again with more specific questions in mind. (These questions will change in each of the next four chapters.)* ***Where did I experience joyful connection today? With others? With you? Where did I remember you were with me? Where did I receive your love? Where did I experience ruptures today? Do I need to do any repair work?***
- *Talk with Jesus about what you discover. What does Jesus celebrate with you? What does he grieve with you?*
- *Ask him for what you want: to grow your capacity for joy, to open your eyes to see joyful connection with others, to offer joyful connection to the people you love, to have more awareness of Jesus with you through your day. (These suggestions will change in each of the next four chapters, but feel free to ask Jesus for whatever you desire.)*
- *Think about what you know about your day tomorrow. What do you want to ask Jesus for?*

CHAPTER 10

WALKING WITH JESUS: BUILDING INTIMACY & INDEPENDENCE

While we were writing this book, friends loaned us their house in the Northwoods of Wisconsin. We needed to get away from distractions and focus on writing. While we were there, our younger son, Tennyson, called to tell us about the first day of his new internship. I (Cyd) went for a walk while talking to him. After we said goodbye, I headed back to the house. But after thirty minutes of walking, I realized I didn't recognize anything. I started to wonder if I was going the wrong way.

Sure enough, when I checked my location on my phone, the little blue dot was not at all where I thought it would be. Because I had been so caught up in my phone call, I had missed a turn. Instead of walking east, I had been walking south for the last half hour. It was only when I checked my location that I recognized how far off track I was.

Jesus is like that blue dot on the map. Jesus locates us, showing us where we really are. Jesus knows where we are and knows the way to life. Jesus meets us where we are and helps move us in the right direction.

This meeting and moving is what Jesus meant by "repent and believe." We might be happily going about our lives in a particular direction, caught up in our surroundings. But then something doesn't seem quite right. Something is off. Jesus locates us, and we recognize we're not where we want or need to be. So we make a change.

After his baptism and time of testing in the wilderness, Jesus began his ministry—his mission to help everyone become deeply attached to God—by proclaiming, "Repent and believe the good news!" (Mark 1:15).

It's possible that the word *repent* feels negative to you. Maybe it is wrapped up in feelings of shame and guilt. Maybe it is connected to spiritual abuse or heavy-handed discipleship. But at its most basic, repentance means recognizing and naming where you are and owning that it's not where you need to be. Repentance is about noticing how sin has shaped the environments you grew up in and owning your responsibility in shaping sinful environments for others. We have all been impacted by fearful survival strategies and protective reactions. All of us have pursued protection over connection in ways that have hurt and harmed others. Repentance is the willingness to expose our survival strategies for what they are and admit they aren't bringing us the life that God intends for us in the Pasture of Joy and Peace.

So Jesus calls us to repent. He shows us where our little blue location dots actually are and invites us to follow him, our Good Shepherd, by changing our minds and our direction. Jesus invites us to turn from our sinful survival strategies and follow him into the Pasture. Jesus calls us to believe in him, to trust him as our attachment figure, and to find security in the family of God.

But how does this happen?

Jesus, in his humanity, models what it looks like to live in intimacy and independence with God. In his divinity, Jesus meets us in our insecure survival strategies and moves us toward an integration of intimacy and independence.

Modeling Intimacy and Independence

Jesus spent his life on earth modeling for us the integration of intimacy and independence. He maintained an intimate relationship with God, his Father in heaven, even while being on an adventure away from God's immediate presence.

If we look at Mark 1:35-39, we can see a great example of this integration:

> Very early in the morning, while it was still dark, Jesus got up, *left the house* and went off to a solitary place, where he prayed. Simon and his companions went to look for him, and when they found him, they exclaimed: "Everyone is looking for you!"
>
> Jesus replied, "Let us go somewhere else—to the nearby villages—so I can preach there also. That is why *I have come*." So he traveled throughout Galilee, preaching in their synagogues and driving out demons.

Let's look at the two phrases we emphasized. In English, "left the house" and "I have come" look pretty different. One is about leaving, and the other is about coming. But in Greek, they are the same word. Because English uses different phrases for exiting and entering a place, we lose the parallelism between the two activities. Mark, the Gospel writer, uses the same Greek word to talk about what Jesus is doing. And we need to pay attention to that.

The first time the word is used, we see that Jesus *went out* to pray in a solitary place. Here Jesus is seeking *intimacy* with the Father. The second time the word is used, Jesus is reminding his disciples that he *came out* to usher in the Kingdom of God. This is Jesus practicing *independence* on behalf of the mission of God. These activities express the two dimensions of intimacy and independence. They are like two sides of Jesus' one attachment relationship with the Father.

We could put it like this:

- Jesus left the house to pray (intimacy).
- And he left heaven to preach (independence).
- Jesus came out for his morning devotions (intimacy).
- And he came down to offer deliverance (independence).
- Jesus went out early to rest (intimacy).
- And he went out into the day to rescue (independence).

In his humanity, Jesus is modeling for us what it looks like to have God as our attachment figure, our safe haven and secure base. Jesus moves toward God as his refuge (intimacy) but also takes on his own responsibility (independence).

But in his divinity, Jesus calls the disciples—and all of us—to be attached to him. When Jesus called the twelve disciples, he was inviting them into a life that builds both intimacy and independence, a life deeply attached to himself.

But first, they would need to become aware of their distorted defaults, lay down their survival strategies, and pick up new thrival skills.

Running New Experiments

As we talked about in chapter 4, our working models of the world—our attachment defaults—were formed by running little experiments in the world. These experiments produced attachment data, which prompted us to create survival strategies specific to our environments. Jesus' call to repent and believe is a call to run new attachment experiments, but now with God at the center. Our attachment defaults don't just magically change to faith, hope, and love because we want them to or even because we read a book about changing them!

You got into your survival strategies with the help of others, and the only way out is with the help of others. You got into your Jungle of Anxiety or Desert of Avoidance by running experiments of intimacy and independence with others. And our defaults will change only by running similar experiments and collecting new data.

Because each of the disciples had lived in a world full of ruptures, they had all developed survival skills specific to their environments. In order for them to change their defaults, Jesus needed to offer them opportunities to collect new data. Through reading about what they experienced, we can collect some new data for ourselves. As we continue through the book, we'll offer practices for you to experiment with in order to collect experiential data.

The Disciples Are Called to the Same Intimacy and Independence

In Mark 3:14-15 we read that Jesus "appointed twelve that they might *be with him* and that he might *send them out*" (emphasis added).

Jesus wanted the disciples to be with him. This means they were to pursue intimacy with Jesus. He spent loads of quality time with his disciples: eating, celebrating, traveling, and talking as they walked.

Jesus also sent the disciples out, training them to take independent action. He sent them off in pairs to go and do everything he had taught them to do. When they had the opportunity to preach or drive out a demon, they didn't go back to Jesus and ask him what to say. They just did it—acting independently in the ways Jesus had taught them.

Because they had spent time with Jesus (intimacy), they knew his heart for people, and they felt the freedom to act in the authority he had given them (independence). Out of love for Jesus they used their independence not for themselves but for the freedom and healing of all those they encountered.

Jesus was inviting his disciples into new experiments of intimacy and independence, helping them grow more deeply attached to God. As we are also disciples of Jesus, we have a lot to learn from these experiments—not only to collect data from the experience of the first disciples but also to conduct similar experiments in our lives.

Faith Is Spelled R-I-S-K

We are part of the Vineyard movement. John Wimber, who started this association of churches in the 1980s, had a motto that has shaped the movement ever since. He said that faith is spelled R-I-S-K. For Wimber, faith in Jesus is not just about what we think or say. It is about what we do. What we do is take risks of faith. We risk loving our neighbors and our enemies. Risk praying for healing. Risk hoping for a miracle. Risk forgiving a painful betrayal. Risk turning the other cheek. Risk looking foolish.

Taking risks of faith, which is sometimes called obedience, is what we mean by running new attachment experiments. Jesus is calling us, like his first disciples, to himself (to grow our capacity for intimacy) and sending us out (to grow our capacity for independence). But these capacities will only grow as we run new attachment experiments in our ordinary lives.

It is only by taking risks of faith that we become deeply attached to Jesus. When we run new attachment experiments, we find that Jesus is meeting us in our survival strategies and moving us toward the Pasture.

GOD'S REPAIR

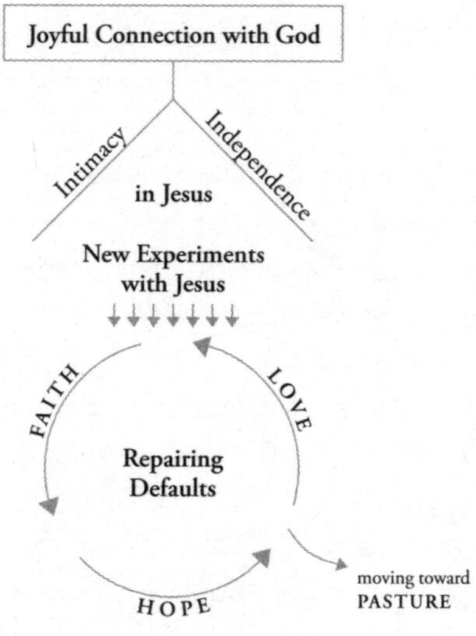

Meeting and Moving the Disciples

Let's look at three episodes of Jesus meeting his first disciples in their insecurity and moving them deeper into a secure attachment with himself.

Refuge: Safety with Jesus (Mark 4:35-41)

Jesus and his disciples are on a boat in the Sea of Galilee. A storm comes up, threatening to drown everyone and putting the disciples in protection mode. Jesus, however, is asleep.

Jesus, in his humanity, is modeling what being deeply attached to God looks like. Even in the midst of a storm, Jesus has faith that God is always available when needed. And knowing that the world is fundamentally a safe place, Jesus is full of hope and can sleep at ease.

But the disciples aren't there yet.

Full of fear, they wake Jesus, shouting, "Teacher, don't you care that we're going to drown?" (verse 38, NLT). They fear for their lives. But not just for their lives. In following Jesus, deep desires have been awakened—the desire for joyful connection, the desire that God might actually be available to them. So they don't just fear for their lives. They fear being abandoned and rejected again. This is why they ask if Jesus even cares if they live or die. They want to know if Jesus is as attached to them as they are beginning to be to him.

In the storm, Jesus, in his divinity, meets them as their Good Shepherd. And he also moves them. First, he silences and stills the storm. In this way, Jesus is meeting their need, meeting them in their insecurity, in their distress. Deeper still, he meets them at their most fundamental question: *Will someone be available to me in my distress?* In calming the storm outside, Jesus also answers the storm inside, the storm caused by their insecure attachment strategies. Jesus meets them in their anxious Jungles and avoidant Deserts.

But Jesus also moves the disciples forward, pressing them with two questions of his own: "Why are you afraid? Do you still have no faith?" (verse 40, NLT).

Jesus does not fault them because they asked for help. They needed help. They needed the help that only God could give. It is never wrong to ask for help when you really need it. But Jesus is putting his finger on their distorted defaults, pointing at their fear and lack of faith. Jesus is pressing them to move deeper in faith, a faith that overcomes fear, a faith that will help them pursue connection over protection.

Seeing Jesus calm the storm starts to shift the disciples' mental models, repairing their insecure attachments. "Who is this man?" they ask. "Even the wind and waves obey him!" (verse 41, NLT). The disciples would know from the Old Testament that it is God alone who commands the winds and the waves, even parting the Red Sea and the Jordan River (see Psalm 18:15; 104:7; 106:9). In awe, they are beginning to see Jesus more and more as their divine attachment figure, as God who has come to rescue them.

In this episode, Jesus reveals that he is not like the come-and-go god found in the Jungle of Anxiety. He's not like the distant-and-aloof god found in the Desert of Avoidance. Jesus leads us to the green pastures as "God with us." In the language of attachment, Jesus reveals himself as our safe haven, as our wise and strong attachment figure, the one protecting us from the storm. Jesus is moving the disciples toward greater faith in himself, the one who is available to calm any storm, the one who has agency to command even the wind and the waves. Jesus is calling them to become more deeply attached to him, the Good Shepherd of their faith.

Jesus offers us rescue and refuge. He offers us intimacy with God. But Jesus also gives us roles and responsibilities, which is independence alongside God. This is the theme of the next episode.

Responsibility: Sent by Jesus (Luke 10:1-20)

As we saw earlier, when Jesus called the twelve disciples, it was to be with him (intimacy) and to be sent out from him (independence). After a certain amount of training, where Jesus models for the disciples what Kingdom ministry looks like, Jesus sends the disciples out in groups of two. This is an opportunity for them to grow in their independence. While in the previous episode Jesus acted like a refuge for the disciples (safe haven), now he is giving them Kingdom responsibility (secure base).

After some time of independent action, the disciples return to Jesus. They have grown so much in confidence and courage through this experience of independence that they shout, "Lord, even the demons obey us when we use your name!" (verse 17, NLT). This is similar to what we see in young children who return from being away from home, wanting to tell what they have done or show Mom and Dad what they have made.

So Jesus meets them like an attuned parent. He meets them in their growing confidence of independence, an independence offered on behalf of others. Jesus even seeks to grow their confidence when he says, "Look, I have given you authority over all the power of the enemy, and you can walk among snakes and scorpions and crush them. Nothing will injure you" (verses 18-19, NLT). That is quite a promise. Whenever we see Jesus talking about how he has given power and authority to the disciples to do something, we can always understand this as Jesus offering Kingdom responsibility through independent agency. This is Jesus restoring the image of God in us, the good design of using our independent agency for the sake of others.

Having been given Kingdom responsibility, and having practiced it through their own agency, the disciples learn they can offer others the refuge that Jesus brings, the peace and freedom that come in the name of Jesus. They are rejoicing in the responsible use of their independence. They have conducted new experiments and have collected new data. Their internal working models are shifting.

But Jesus also moves the disciples forward. He does this by moving the focus from independence and placing it back on intimacy. Jesus reminds the disciples, "Don't rejoice because evil spirits obey you; rejoice because your names are registered in heaven" (verse 20, NLT). In other words, rejoice in the intimacy you have with God, not just in the independence you have alongside God. Jesus meets them in their joy and moves them deeper into joy, the joy of intimacy with God.

In this episode, we see how Jesus meets us not just in our weaknesses but also in our strengths. Jesus affirms what we are good at and what we accomplish. But even in meeting us there, he wants to move us deeper. In our independent action, Jesus wants to be sure we don't lose sight of intimacy with him. And in our intimacy with him, he wants to be sure we don't forget we are empowered for independent action alongside him.

Take Courage: Peter Walks on Water (Matthew 14:22-33)

The last episode to look at is Peter walking on water. Telling the disciples to go without him across the lake, Jesus stays on the shore to pray. But then he goes out to them, walking on the water. The bewildered disciples think Jesus is a ghost. So he shouts to them, "Take courage. I am here!" (verse 27, NLT).

Peter, taking courage just as Jesus said, decides to try something crazy. It is the kind of crazy attachment experiment we all need to start doing more, an experiment that integrates intimacy and independence. Peter is letting his faith be spelled R-I-S-K. He wants to walk on the water (independence) in order to go to Jesus (intimacy). In a very real way, Peter, in his toddling discipleship, is trying to walk, taking his first big steps of attachment faith toward Jesus. Peter is trying to build and integrate his capacity for intimacy and independence. Peter is learning to become deeply attached to God.

So Jesus meets Peter in his courage and boldness (independence) and tells Peter to come to him (intimacy). Getting out of the boat, Peter starts walking on the water toward Jesus. In this moment, walking on the water, Peter is integrating intimacy with God and independence alongside God. He is living and acting just how God created us to be.

But then Peter looks away. He takes his eyes off Jesus. Peter sees the wind and the waves and becomes terrified. He starts to sink. Peter is at war with himself. On the one hand, Peter's old survival strategies are kicking in, his old understanding of how the world works. They tell him to be afraid, to protect instead of connect. On the other hand, his new attachment to Jesus causes him to shout, "Save me, Lord!" (verse 30, NLT). Peter is learning that Jesus is available when he is in distress. That's why Peter had the courage to attempt walking on the water in the first place.

When Peter is looking at Jesus, living out of a deep attachment to Jesus, he can walk on the water to Jesus. But when Peter looks away, living out of his old attachment strategies, he falters and sinks. "Why did you doubt me?" Jesus asks Peter (verse 31, NLT).

The question is the same for us: Are you looking at Jesus, or something else? Are you deeply attached to the Good Shepherd, or insecurely attached to (or detached from) someone else?

Gathering New Data of Intimacy and Independence

Just as Jesus offered the disciples the opportunity to run new experiments with him as their attachment figure, so he offers us the same invitation. Jesus, in his humanity, models how to live in intimacy and independence with God. In our independence, we can take action to imitate him. But Jesus isn't just our model. In his divinity, he is also our new attachment figure. We can't rewrite our defaults just by following his example. Our defaults can be rewritten only when we lean into the intimacy he offers us.

Jesus is our Good Shepherd. He loves us first, and because of his love, we can respond to him in love by running new experiments and collecting new data about how he is available and intimate, as well as how we are equipped and empowered to independently work alongside him for the coming of the Kingdom of God.

Practice: Examen of Intimacy and Independence

- *Begin by taking a couple of deep breaths—in through your nose and out through your mouth. As you do this, remember God's gladness to be with you, no matter how you enter this time. Ask the Holy Spirit to help you notice what you need to notice.*
- *Next, recall your day in the order in which it happened, with an eye toward finding the good things.*
- *Now thank God for these things. Appreciate them as specific gifts, expressions of God's care for you.*
- *Now review the day again with more specific questions in mind:* **Where did I experience intimacy today? With others? With Jesus? Where did I experience Jesus meeting me today? Where did I practice independence? Where does it feel like Jesus is moving me today? Where did I experience ruptures today? Do I need to do any repair work?**
- *Talk with Jesus about what you discover. What does Jesus celebrate with you? What does he grieve with you?*
- *Ask him for what you want: to grow in integrating intimacy and independence; to offer intimacy and independence to others. (Feel free to ask Jesus for whatever you desire.)*
- *Think about what you know about your day tomorrow. What do you want to ask Jesus for?*

CHAPTER 11

TESTED WITH JESUS: FORMING FAITH, HOPE & LOVE

Things seemed better before she was baptized.

Monica was in her early forties. She already had a few kids, a successful career, and had been married for almost twenty years. She had spent years exploring faith before she decided it was time to make a commitment and be baptized.

It was a thrilling day! Family, friends, and her new church community gathered to witness her baptism and to celebrate her entrance into the family of God. She was full of joy and excitement, relieved to finally be on the other side of this decision she had contemplated for years.

About a week later, things were falling apart. Her husband was having difficulty at work and taking it out on the family. One of her kids was exhibiting signs of mental instability. Her own work was unraveling. Her dog got sick, and things around the house started to break down all at once.

As she talked about it all, she said, "Things were much better before I was baptized!"

Monica isn't the first person to feel this way. We've seen similar experiences and heard similar statements from many people who have been newly baptized. We baptized seven teenagers in our youth group one Easter Sunday, and about two weeks later, each of them was having a hard time.

It's a common occurrence, and it's often explained in one of two ways. Either your expectations of how life was going to change were unrealistic and you're dealing with the disappointment of unmet expectations, or you've declared allegiance with God, and Satan has unleashed his forces to tempt you to change sides again.

In one case, you (or your high expectations) are the problem. In the other case, Satan is the problem.

But what if this common experience isn't a problem at all? What if God is using this experience to grow you into the new family you've just been baptized into?

We looked at the baptism of Jesus as a foundational moment of joyful connection—a highly relational encounter with Father and Spirit. It's a real feel-good moment.

But what comes next in the life of Jesus? Jesus goes into the wilderness and faces temptation. He is tested. Just as the shepherd David learned to fight off bears and lions in the fields before facing Goliath, so too Jesus, our Good Shepherd, goes into the wilderness to fight against the temptations of the devil before facing and defeating the sin of the world.

Testing and Attacking Attachment

We often hear about these three temptations as the devil trying to get Jesus to sin. In sermons and books, these three temptations are thought to stand for the three typical ways that all people are tempted by sin to distort the human needs for provision, protection, and purpose apart from God.[1]

But what if, instead of tempting Jesus toward sin, the devil is attacking Jesus at a deeper level? What if Jesus is being tested at the level of his attachment defaults? And what if Jesus is modeling for us the repair of our ruptured attachment defaults, helping us return to faith, hope, and love?

As a reminder, here are the three attachment defaults we covered in chapter 4.

- *Are others* available *when I'm in distress?*
- *Will this distress be* alleviated*?*
- *How do I use my* agency *amid distress?*

The only way the devil can derail Jesus' mission is to attack his secure attachment.

In his temptations, Jesus is not only modeling, in his humanity, how to defend ourselves against attachment attacks. Jesus is also, in his divinity, repairing our attachment defaults so that we can grow in faith, hope, and love.

First Testing: Stones to Bread and Attacking Hope

In chapter 4 we talked about the defaults in a particular order because they tend to develop that way in childhood. In reality, they are all connected and reinforce one another. When Satan tempts Jesus, he attacks each one of them, but he picks on the second default first. This makes sense, because when we are in distress and facing difficult circumstances, our attachment system becomes activated. It's through the distress and the experience of discomfort that we then want to know if someone is available. *Is the world good? Or is it out to get me?* So, like all of us, Satan attacks Jesus at the level of distress first, which means attacking the second attachment default, "Will this distress be alleviated?" This default is focused on how we see the world around us. Satan is attacking hope.

Let's look at this testing more closely. After Jesus had been fasting for forty days and was famished, Satan says, "If you are the Son of God, tell these stones to become loaves of bread" (Matthew 4:3, NLT).

First, notice the devil attacking with a question about Jesus' attachment relationship with God. "If you are the Son of God" is a challenge to the joyful connection Jesus has with the Father. The devil is trying to create doubt about whether the Father is really attached and attuned to Jesus. The devil is saying, "If you're so connected, so loved and delighted in, why are you hungry? If you are the Son of God, demand that this distress be relieved."

Satan is trying to push Jesus into protection mode. He's trying to get Jesus to solve his own problems, to do what needs to be done to ensure his survival—apart from his relationship to God. Satan is urging Jesus to take matters into his own hands rather than waiting expectantly for God's relief.

Second, notice the devil is focusing on Jesus' basic needs. After fasting for forty days, Jesus is uncomfortable when the devil comes to him. We've already talked about our nervous systems and how we have two different priorities embedded in our bodies: connect or protect. When our bodies experience any kind of threat—like hunger—we shift from connection to protection. We do what we need to do to survive. Jesus is hungry. His human body naturally wants to do what is needed to survive.

When we are uncomfortable, it's instinctive to switch into protection mode.

Fraud Alert

Geoff and I experienced this in a major way in 2021. We got scammed by a sophisticated fraud ring and ended up losing a substantial amount of money (yup, we are those people). The saga stretched out for a few months, and every step of the way, we experienced more and more distress. At the same time, Geoff's mother was succumbing to a two-year battle with cancer. It was a very difficult time.

In moments like this, it is easy to lose connection as a priority—with God, with others, with our own emotions and thought processes. It's easy to ask: Will this ever go away? Will this distress be alleviated? Is there anyone who will help me? Is God even there?

My primary attachment strategies spring from the Jungle. So when I'm in distress, I watch my people for nonverbal communication, throw rules out the window, rely on others to help me stay calm, and assume that whatever has gone wrong is my fault. So in this financial fraud distress, I blamed myself, and I wanted to spend time with Geoff. I wanted to make sure we were connected and on the same page about things. I wanted to talk about it a lot, process my emotions, and be together in it so that I wouldn't suffer alone. I wanted to know if he thought it was my fault. And I wanted to do what I could to reduce his suffering—so I could feel better.

Meanwhile, Geoff's primary attachment strategies spring from the Desert. He prioritizes verbal-logical-linear communication, rules over relationships, and an overreliance on solving problems alone, and he tends to blame others when things aren't going well. So during this stressful season, he was using a lot of energy to maintain independence, stay in his head, and be rational about it all. He wanted to spend more time by himself, watching sports or reading books.

Our strategies were clashing. We were just trying to survive. Valuing intimacy, I wanted to spend *more* time together. Valuing independence, he wanted *less* time together. He wanted to keep his emotions inside, and I wanted to process them all the time. I was trying to fix the discomfort; he was trying to ignore it. I felt abandoned and let down by him; he felt nagged and smothered by me.

We had shifted into protection mode and had to put a lot of effort into staying connected. We were each pulling from our lopsided survival strategies.

This is exactly what the devil is hoping to accomplish in testing a very hungry Jesus. He tries to shift Jesus from connection to protection. "Is this world really safe, or is it savage? Is this world a home, or is it hazardous? Is your hungry body blessed, or is it broken?"

But rather than living from the Jungle, the Desert, or the War Zone, Jesus handles this moment using the integrated strategies of the Pasture.

Answering the First Testing: Connection over Protection

Jesus answers, "The Scriptures say, 'People do not live by bread alone, but by every word that comes from the mouth of God'" (Matthew 4:4, NLT).

Notice that Jesus responds in an integrated way. He uses his cognitive tools to remember a passage of Scripture that he had probably memorized when he was young. Remembering these words helps him reframe the situation and gain a perspective beyond the discomfort of the moment.

But he also draws on emotional resources by focusing on his relationship with God. He is reminding the devil (and himself, and us) that life is not only about physical needs but is also about living in connection with God.

Jesus keeps himself from being pushed into protection mode by remembering that the fullness of life comes from connection to God, not seeking protection in or from the world. Just like an infant needs relational care as much as or more than physical care, Jesus reminds the devil that he trusts the relational words of his Father will relieve all distress.

What, exactly, are the words that come from the mouth of God?

Jesus probably still has the words from his baptism ringing in his ears, when the Father said, "You are my dearly loved Son, and you bring me great joy." Jesus is recalling that his connection with the Father is much more important than his physical needs.

Basically, Jesus responds to the devil's temptation by saying, "Because I am attached to God, this distress is not enough to become a rupture between my Father and me." In his humanity, Jesus models how to resist the temptation to question whether his distress would be alleviated.

Restored Default: Jesus Is Our Hope

In his divinity, Jesus does much more than model how to hope. He himself *is* our hope!

We can't hope that this world will never bring distress. We can't hope that we'll get through life with everything going our way. We will face hunger, financial stress, loss, and all sorts of environmental and circumstantial distress. In these moments, we may be tempted to think the world is against us. We may try to protect ourselves by looking for ways to turn stones to bread.

But we are not left alone to alleviate our distress. Jesus, our Good Shepherd, has authority over all the world. He walks on water, silences wind and rain, restores broken bodies, opens blind eyes, and crosses cultural boundaries. Jesus even overcomes death.

The distress of the world can never overshadow the reality that Jesus is the relief for all our distress. He is our refuge and our hope. Jesus is the repair of all our ruptures. He sees our distress. He hears our cries of discomfort. He understands how we suffer. And he comes to be with us, to act on our behalf. He is our Good Shepherd, and he *will* lead us into his house forever. We can depend on him and wait expectantly for him, even in distress.

Whether we are in the Jungle, Desert, or War Zone, Jesus meets us where we are.

Hope like Jesus

Because of the connection/protection priority designed into our nervous system, we are regularly faced with the temptation to be undone by distress. When Monica was facing her husband's distress, the confusion around her child's mental health, her own work stress, and a sick dog on top of it all, it was easy for her to doubt that following Jesus was a good idea.

But Monica spoke up about her distress. She dared to say, "Everything seems harder since I was baptized." And so we were able to help her reframe her distress. She had already been memorizing some of God's words in the Bible, and we could help her identify passages that were especially helpful in reminding herself of the power and authority of God as well as the love of God.

We could also offer her some nonverbal tools, using her imagination and memory to revisit a place of calm and safety. From this place of connection priority in her nervous system, she could talk with Jesus about the distress she was experiencing. And he could affirm his desire to be with her and to care for her.

Monica also had to come to terms with her expectation that things would be automatically better once she committed to following Jesus. She became more aware of how much hope she was putting in her husband's ability to handle his emotions, the well-being of her kids, her competency at her job, and the comfort of her dog. She started praying that Jesus would be her hope. Using integrated tools, Monica could continue in the life the Good Shepherd was inviting her into.

And this hope is essentially what sustained us in that crazy fraud experience. Even though the mismatch of our early attachment strategies made things difficult, we were able to come together and use some of the integrated skills we've grown in as we've grown in our attachment. We could remember joyful connection with God and with one another. We drew on our familiarity with Scripture and reminded each other of the reality that relationship with God is bigger than all of this. This, too, would pass. And the relationship with God and living Jesus' life together is much more essential than the money we lost. This cannot destroy our hope.

In all these ways, while Jesus was meeting us in our distress, he was also moving us toward hope and deeper into the Pasture.

Second Testing: Jumping from the Temple and Attacking Faith

The devil's next attack on Jesus targets his relationship default, the default focused on whether others are available. Satan is now attempting to get Jesus to maximize intimacy and become hypervigilant about his relationship with God.

> Then the devil took him to the holy city, Jerusalem, to the highest point of the Temple, and said, "If you are the Son of God, jump off! For the Scriptures say,
>
> 'He will order his angels to protect you.
> And they will hold you up with their hands
> so you won't even hurt your foot on a stone.'"
>
> MATTHEW 4:5-6, NLT

Using words from Psalm 91, Satan is trying to push Jesus into testing the availability of God. "Is God really here for you? Does God care? Can you trust your Father? Will your Father catch you if you jump? Should you really have faith in God?"

Satan is trying to hyperactivate Jesus' attachment system. He is trying to lead Jesus into a Jungle way of living. "Be on high alert! Watch your relationships at all times! Test your safety net!" Rather than living an integrated life that connects past and present, rules and relationships, reliable patterns and unique people, Satan is tempting Jesus to live a disintegrated and lopsided life focused only on intimacy with God.

Jesus is being tempted to enter the Jungle. Tempted to live as a self-needing-others rather than a self-with-others. Tempted to live from a distorted sense of faith and trust.

Testing the Relationship: Jungle Response

When Geoff and I were first married, one of my survival strategies was exposed. We called it "speaking into the air."

I would be bothered by something or need something and would say something indirect about it: "It sure would be nice if I could walk into a clean kitchen after work." "Wow! The laundry is overflowing!"

One day, Geoff asked, "How do you expect me to respond to that?"

I was stumped. I had literally never thought about it. What *was* I expecting? Did I expect Geoff to immediately clean the kitchen? Was I demanding an explanation as to why he hadn't done the laundry when he had offered to?

Geoff encouraged me, "If you want something, ask. But don't just 'speak into the air.'"

Once he had called my attention to it, I started noticing just how often I did it, and I got curious about why.

Here's how the survival strategy seemed to go:

- *I need something.*
- *If I ask for it directly, he might say no.*
- *If I just speak it into the air, he will hear me.*
- *If he cares about me, he will respond in a way that demonstrates he cares—and I didn't even have to ask!*
- *If he doesn't respond, it's okay, because I didn't ask for anything.*

I could be safe from hurt or rejection because I didn't actually ask. This was me, living from my *maybe*, testing the relationship. I was falling directly into Satan's second temptation.

Truth is, I had been doing the same thing with God! I never asked for anything specific. As long as I just sort of spoke into the air, then if God cared, God could respond. I didn't have to feel rejected if my prayers went unanswered because I hadn't actually asked for anything. I was implicitly asking the same questions Satan was tempting Jesus to ask his Father: "Do you care? Are you available to me? Do you love me?"

Answering the Second Temptation: Trusting the Relationship

But Jesus, in his humanity, doesn't fall into the trap. He doesn't need to test the relationship. He has already collected so much data about God's availability and his belonging that Jesus doesn't need to wonder. Jesus simply answers Satan, "It is also written: 'Do not put the LORD your God to the test'" (Matthew 4:7).

Jesus will not let a moment of distress overshadow years of trust. He's not going to hyperactivate his attachment and test the relationship. Instead, he again uses the integrated tools of the Pasture. By quoting Deuteronomy 6:16 to answer Satan, Jesus is pulling from his cognitive tool kit. Jesus is remembering the words that God gave Israel when they were tempted to forget how God saved them from slavery in Egypt and fed them with manna and gave them water in the wilderness. Israel needed to remember all the relational data they had collected about God's faithfulness and not put God through more tests. In the same way, Jesus remembers all the relational data he has collected and refuses to test God more. When we are tempted to focus on whether people are available in the present, we need to look to the past and see the patterns of faithfulness.

Restored Default: Jesus Is Our Faith

In his humanity, Jesus models what faith in God looks like. He models how the mental model of others and their availability, our designed default, is supposed to look. We can rest secure in God, living at peace in our connection without resorting to protective strategies that constantly test relationships.

In his divinity, Jesus is the one we put our faith in. He is our Good Shepherd. He knows us, calls us by name, and lays down his life for us (see John 10:14-18, 25-30). Jesus doesn't just *tell* us that he cares and is available. He *demonstrates* that he is trustworthy. We can put our faith and trust in Jesus because he has claimed us as his own.

As Jesus repairs our distorted defaults, let us move from our anxious Jungles and avoidant Deserts where we test whether God is really for us and with us and settle into a place of peace and rest, having faith in the one who is faithful to us.

Third Testing: "Worship Me" and Attacking Love

The devil's last attack on Jesus targets how he views himself, the default focused on agency. Since trying to hyperactivate Jesus' attachment system toward intimacy didn't work, the devil flips the strategy. Maybe he can push Jesus into deactivating his attachment system and focusing only on his independence. He wants Jesus to use his agency for his own glory, purposes, and goals.

> The devil took him to the peak of a very high mountain and showed him all the kingdoms of the world and their glory. "I will give it all to you," he said, "if you will kneel down and worship me."
>
> MATTHEW 4:8-9, NLT

"Why be so focused on the Father's will and the Father's plan? Why not be your own man with your own plan?" asks the tempter. Satan knows that Jesus is focused on repairing a ruptured world, on gathering all the lost sheep, no matter the cost. He's tempting Jesus into practicing independence devoid of intimacy. He's inviting Jesus to be king without having to follow anyone else or submit to the Father's plan. It's a classic temptation to allow the ends to justify the means. "If you get the power, fame, and glory, does it really matter *how* you get it?" Jesus is being tempted toward the love of self, separated from the love of others.

Jesus is being tempted to enter the Desert. Tempted to live as a self-without-others. Tempted to live from a distorted sense of love.

Testing Agency: Desert Response

Like the rest of the world, we've fallen in love with pickleball. We figured out that we could squeeze a portable pickleball court onto our driveway, so now we head out and hit the ball back and forth when we need a break (including from writing this book—no joke). This, of course, is just another excuse for my (Geoff's) natural competitiveness. Sometimes this comes out as me giving too much advice to Cyd about how she can improve. She needs to improve because we need to be better than all the other couples we play!

This competitive streak also reaches into other areas of my life, usually expressed as *compulsive comparison*. How are my adult children doing compared to others? Am I more or less out of shape than another guy my age? How is our book selling compared to that other book? Did we get as many speaking engagements as that other couple?

While I was working on my doctorate, I often compared myself to other students. What grades were they getting? Were they presenting papers at a conference? Was it a national conference or just a local conference? How many peer-reviewed articles had they published? After I finished my PhD, I would compare myself to other academics, and if I didn't measure up, then I would tell myself I wasn't as old as them and would catch up soon, or I would spiritualize the comparison and remind myself I was both a pastor and a professor, so I couldn't be expected to produce as much as full-time professors.

As one who comes from the Desert, the temptation is to compare my success to the successes of others. Is my kingdom as famous as that person's kingdom? Is my popularity as big as theirs? Does my podcast have as many listeners as that other one? Living in comparison with others tempts me toward self-love instead of love of God and love of others. Living in comparison leads me toward competition instead of collaboration. This competition and comparison, where I try to build my own self-without-others, is a distortion of my sense of agency. It emphasizes my independence at the expense of intimacy with God and others. God wants us to creatively use our agency for love of others. But Satan tempts us to use our agency for ourselves.

Answering the Third Temptation

In his humanity, Jesus models for us how to resist this temptation. Our agency is not about power, fame, glory, or status. It's not about getting what you want when you want it, no matter the cost.

Jesus answers this temptation with "The Scriptures say, 'You must worship the LORD your God and serve only him'" (Matthew 4:10, NLT).

To worship God and serve God alone is another way of saying that we are to love God. Jesus answers that he will not deactivate his attachment system to achieve his own goals. He will not pursue independence at the expense of intimacy.

Jesus models that the right response to God's availability and God's alleviation is to take action aligned with God's love. God loves the world and wants to repair it. God loves people and wants to repair the rupture between God and humanity. Jesus is taking independent action aligned with the Father's love.

Jesus' sense of self is "self-with-others." He knows he is loved by the Father, and out of the overflow of the Father's love, Jesus loves the world enough to resist any temptation to take shortcuts or aim for his own glory. By integrating independence and intimacy, Jesus will keep his attachment relationship and use it to serve others. He uses his agency to bless others, not bless himself. He uses his agency to connect with others, not protect himself. Jesus models love in response to the Father's love.

Restored Default: Jesus Is Love

But Jesus doesn't just model what it looks like to love. Jesus, in his divinity, *is* love.

We might paraphrase Paul's description of love in 1 Corinthians 13:4-7 like this:

> *Jesus* is patient and kind. *Jesus* is not jealous or boastful or proud or rude. He does not demand his own way. He is not irritable, and he keeps no record of being wronged. *Jesus* does not rejoice about injustice but rejoices whenever the truth wins out. *Jesus* never gives up, never loses faith, is always hopeful, and endures through every circumstance.

Jesus uses his agency not only to love the Father but to love us, his sheep. Jesus offers us love in action. "There is no greater love than to lay down one's life for one's friends" (John 15:13, NLT).

Love like Jesus

Without Jesus, we are incapable of loving in any way other than to serve ourselves. We will say we love others when we are actually pursuing intimacy to quiet our anxiety. We will say we love others when we are really protecting our independence to satisfy our avoidance.

We are designed to overflow in love toward God and others. When we are filled with the love of God, we can freely give it away to others. This is what our agency is for: loving God and loving others. Our agency isn't only for pursuing our own interests. It's also for pursuing what is best for others. It isn't for circling the wagons of our self-protective survival strategies. It's also for ensuring the weak are protected. Our agency is designed for love in action.

After facing these temptations, Jesus, in his humanity, emerges from the wilderness, having modeled secure attachment with the Father. In his divinity, he has done what Adam and Eve could not do. He has overturned the temptation to sin and has made the way for all of us to become securely attached, even as he is.

Practice: Examen of Defaults

- *Begin by taking a couple of deep breaths—in through your nose and out through your mouth. As you do this, remember God's gladness to be with you, no matter how you enter this time. Ask the Holy Spirit to help you notice what you need to notice.*
- *Next, recall your day in the order in which it happened, with an eye toward finding the good things.*
- *Now thank God for these things. Appreciate them as specific gifts, expressions of God's care for you.*
- *Now review the day again with more specific questions in mind.* ***Where did I experience testing today? How did I respond to the testing? What default answers were revealed in my response? Where did I feel strong in faith today? Where did I exercise hope? Where did I use my agency to love? Where did I experience ruptures today? Do I need to do any repair work?***
- *Talk with Jesus about what you discover. What does Jesus celebrate with you? What does he grieve with you?*
- *Ask him for what you want: to be able to recognize moments of temptation to do things your own way, test relationships, or protect yourself rather than connect with Jesus; to grow in faith, hope, and love; to trust Jesus' availability, hope in his alleviation of distress, and use your agency to love. (Feel free to ask Jesus for whatever you desire.)*
- *Think about what you know about your day tomorrow. What do you want to ask Jesus for?*

CHAPTER 12

DYING WITH JESUS: DECONSTRUCTING DISTORTIONS OF GOD

Opposites attract. Why is this? And what does it have to do with attaching to God?

After a roller-coaster relationship, Emily and Noah got married. But now, after a couple of years and with the pressures of expecting their first child, they aren't sure the relationship is going to make it. What happened?

At the beginning, Emily (a Desert dweller) seemed confident, stable, and predictable to Noah. She had goals, made plans, and stuck to them. Noah (a Jungle dweller) was attracted to this. He liked how she could handle his big emotions without getting too high or low when he was feeling all the feelings. But now Emily seemed more distant and aloof, even critical of Noah all the time. She expected him to fit into all her rules and routines. Noah felt like Emily was pulling away from him. He felt abandoned.

On the opposite side, meeting Noah was a breath of fresh air for Emily, bringing passion and spontaneity into her life. Sure, he was a bit much sometimes, but part of her knew she needed to connect more with the emotional side of life, and Noah helped with that. But now it was overwhelming and exhausting. Noah didn't do what they agreed upon, claiming this or that exception and then doing everything differently. Emily never knew what to expect from Noah and was frustrated that he couldn't just let go of past hurts—whether it was with her, his friends, or his coworkers. Emily constantly felt like Noah was pulling her into his chaos. She felt overwhelmed and smothered.

Emily and Noah had fallen into the Jungle-Desert trap.[1] This kind of relationship experiences short-term gain with long-term pain.

The Desert dweller has a deep but mostly forgotten desire to be welcomed, celebrated, and accepted for who they are, not just what they do. The Desert dweller needs help processing and expressing their social-emotional side. The Jungle dweller has a deep but ignored desire and admiration for stability, consistency, and reliability. They need help regulating their emotions by emphasizing the cognitive side of life. Each is attracted to what they find in the other person and wants to benefit from their strengths. This is the short-term gain.

But this kind of relationship comes with long-term pain. The trouble is that each person's attachment defaults—their implicit ways of processing relationships with others, the world, and themselves—are not miraculously changed by being in a relationship with someone from a different landscape. After a couple of months, years, or decades, the person living in the Jungle will try to get their partner to be more like them. They will wish, cajole, badger, and passive-aggressively try to make them conform to life in the Jungle. But the person living in the Desert will do the same. Both will end up frustrated, feeling rejected and wondering how they got there in the first place.

Each person is unconsciously trying to drag the other into their own insecure landscape.

We do the same thing in our relationship with God.

Remaking God in Our Image

At the beginning of our life with Jesus, it feels like he fills in all the cracks. Where we felt stuck, Jesus showed us a way forward. Where we felt trapped, Jesus gave us freedom. We felt unloved, and Jesus accepted us. In our fear and shame, Jesus gave us forgiveness and love. Jesus compensated for what we didn't have. And this is a good thing. He was meeting us in our insecurity.

But following the Good Shepherd into the Pasture beyond our anxious Jungles and avoidant Deserts is not a straightforward process. It's not like Jesus just meets us where we are and moves us where we need to be overnight. In fact, the process can go in the *reverse* direction. As much as Jesus is *drawing* us into the Pasture, parts of us are *dragging* Jesus into the Jungle, the Desert, or the War Zone.

This is the age-old problem of making God according to our image, but at the attachment level. Deep down, we are so comfortable with our survival strategies, so comfortable living in the Jungle, the Desert, or the War Zone, that it would be terrifying to live anywhere else.

Our attachment strategies helped us survive. But to really thrive in the life Jesus has for us, we need to move beyond these lopsided survival strategies.

This is scary. It might even feel a bit like dying.

A Square Peg in a Round Hole

You've probably heard that we all have a God-shaped hole that only God can fill. This is partially right. It would be better to say that we have an attachment wound that God is healing. The trouble is that instead of letting God heal this wound, we try to fit God into our insecure attachment strategies.

When researchers started connecting attachment theory to religion, they noticed two things.[2] First, in the short-term, during a profound personal crisis, people turned to God as an attachment figure who looked the opposite of their attachment figures and survival strategies. If you were raised in the Desert, then it might be a relief to find out that God is like the Jungle—all relationship with few rules; all affirmation with little challenge; all love without much judgment. At least, that is how you understood the gift of the gospel.

After a lifetime of trying to earn your worth through your work, a Desert dweller would find peace and rest in God's unmerited grace. If you were raised in the Jungle, then it might be a relief to know that God has a sovereign plan, is perfectly in charge, and makes and keeps promises. This would be comforting and peaceful after all the drama in the Jungle. But this only works for a time.

The second finding was that in the long-term, people tended to revert to their older attachment strategies. Over time, people started interacting with God in a way that mirrored their attachment strategies. In romantic relationships, this is why the Jungle-Desert marriage is so difficult. After the excitement of the new wears off, one person secretly tries to drag the other into their attachment landscape. They want the other person's survival skills to correspond to—be like—their own.

We do the same thing with God. We might initially be drawn to God because God has what we are missing. God compensates for what we don't have. But over time, this short-term compensation isn't enough. Our deep attachment system hasn't changed, and we try to fit God into our attachment-shaped hole.

This conflict between our new attachment with God and our old attachment strategies can lead to a crisis of faith. Without knowing it, we might begin to deconstruct everything we have believed about God, even while unconsciously making God correspond to our insecure attachment strategies. Instead of following Jesus into the Pasture of Joy and Peace, we just trade a Jungle god for a Desert god, or a Desert god for a Jungle god. Or we just move between Jungle, Desert, and War Zone.

Hannah never felt close to her father. He was quite successful in his field and always a little disappointed that Hannah didn't follow in his footsteps. That disappointment hovered silently over her well into adulthood. There were verbal declarations of love, but she never really felt it. Later, when Hannah married, she did her best to be a loving spouse and mother and was committed to her church. Hannah was a high-functioning Desert dweller, desperate to feel God's love in a tangible way.

Explicitly—because it is good doctrine, and Desert dwellers are usually committed to good doctrine—she knew that God loved her because God is love (see 1 John 4:8). This compensated for the lack of love she felt in life. But implicitly she responded as if God lived in the Desert, never bringing her big emotions to God (if she allowed herself to feel them at all) and never asking God for help (because she was used to solving her own problems).

After a mild faith crisis and what some call deconstruction, Hannah seemed to have a more relaxed attitude about God and spirituality. The stress of feeling loved by God disappeared. Not that she felt more loved by God. Rather, she decided she didn't need to feel it. Hannah said she realized we don't really need to seek God's will for our lives because God's goal for us is that we learn to grow up and make our own decisions. God doesn't want to control us, she said; God wants us to be free.

While sounding pious and mature, Hannah had actually dragged God into her Desert. Certainly, God doesn't want to control us. But God is seeking collaborators—partners who are in relationship. And yes, God wants us to be free, but not so free that we live as functional atheists going through the religious motions. Hannah had made God into the image of the Desert, where independence is valued over intimacy, where collaboration is viewed as controlling, and where personal responsibility is prized more than relationships.

In the end, Hannah's old attachment strategy won out.

Luke grew up in a military family. There was lots of moving and new people, and little stability and routine. Luke developed a keen eye for the moods and emotions of all around him, always ready to leverage the situation for maximum reward and minimal cost. Scattered between all his relationships and projects, Luke never had a firm sense of self. But in adulthood, he used his Jungle survival skills working sales at a small tech firm. He was quite successful.

Spiritually, Luke had found his way into a liturgical church committed to correct doctrine. The rules, routines, and focus on the life of the mind were a pleasant reprieve from the relational stress and emotional roller coaster that he and his wife—a fellow Jungle dweller—were constantly on. The view of God as sovereign and unchanging and a church that placed emotions under reason perfectly compensated for his chaotic internal life. God was God, and he was not. It was nice for Luke to remember that he wasn't the center of the universe.

But over time Luke felt something was missing. When his children became adults and started rejecting the church's rules, and even rejecting faith, Luke entered a crisis of faith. Luke shifted his theological understanding toward an inclusive God who doesn't really care what we believe or how we act as long as we love one another.

In the end, Luke's old attachment strategy won out. Rather than being drawn deeper into secure attachment with God, he just made God mirror his Jungle attachment.

Dragging Jesus Down

We have already encountered the ups and downs of Peter, the fisherman called to follow Jesus. Like most people in the Bible, we don't have enough information to know if he lived from an anxious Jungle, avoidant Desert, or chaotic War Zone. But we do know that Peter—like Jesus and all the other disciples—grew up under the brutal Roman occupation of Israel, which would have been the kind of environment that could push anyone into the War Zone of conflicting and incoherent attachment strategies. Peter's story reveals the conflict between his new secure attachment to Jesus and his old survival strategies. Peter's ups and downs with Jesus show us the conflict between his explicit desire to follow the Good Shepherd and his implicit attachment defaults.

On one of their trips, Jesus asks the disciples what people are saying about him. But he really wants to know who the disciples think he is. Peter, having watched Jesus closely and comparing him to the Scriptures, answers, "You are the Messiah, the Son of the living God." Jesus responds to this amazing revelation by telling Peter that "upon this rock [Peter] I will build my church, and all the powers of hell will not conquer it" (Matthew 16:16-18, NLT).

Peter is understanding and living into a secure attachment with Jesus.

But then Jesus tells the disciples what it means to be the Messiah. The Son of God will suffer terrible things, die for their salvation, and be raised from the dead. Not only is this talk about death confusing, but it is also distressing. Peter has found Jesus to be everything he has been missing. He has found peace in the presence of Jesus, the one who is stronger and wiser and available. He has found purpose within the heavenly Kingdom Jesus is bringing. All of that is great and amazing. It feels so good. But now Jesus is talking about dying, and this crisis prompts all sorts of fear and anxiety in Peter. All his implicit strategies became explicit.

So Peter responds from his old survival strategies. Peter, unintentionally, wants to drag Jesus into his War Zone. After revealing who Jesus really is, now Peter rebukes Jesus for talking about death. He takes him aside and says, "Heaven forbid, Lord. This will never happen to you!" (Matthew 16:22, NLT). Peter faces a conflict between his expectation of who Jesus should be and what he should do, and what Jesus is claiming to be and do. In protection mode, Peter tries to resolve that conflict by changing Jesus. Instead of living from faith, hope, and love, Peter is dragging Jesus down into his own doubts, despairs, and fears.

But to change Jesus to fit our mental model—to make Jesus fit our Jungle, Desert, or War Zone—is the work of Satan.

Dying with Jesus

And Jesus rebukes Peter accordingly. Refusing to be dragged into Peter's insecure attachment strategies, Jesus says, "Get away from me, Satan! You are a dangerous trap to me. You are seeing things merely from a human point of view, not from God's" (Matthew 16:23, NLT). This human point of view is Peter living from his old attachment strategies, from his distorted defaults. The apostle Paul states the same thing when he says, "To set the mind on the flesh is death, but to set the mind on the Spirit is life and peace" (Romans 8:6, NRSV). This human/fleshly point of view sees the world through distorted attachment defaults and lopsided survival strategies, which are all focused on protection over connection. But God's point of view (the mind set on the Spirit) is repairing ruptures and offering joyful connection at the deepest level, deeper than our most basic survival instinct.

In these two episodes from Peter's life, we see that on the conscious and explicit level, when he doesn't feel distressed, Peter can acknowledge who Jesus really is. But on the unconscious and implicit level, which is activated when distressed, Peter is still living out of his old attachment defaults and insecure survival strategies. Jesus is drawing Peter into a secure attachment.

Jesus, digging even deeper, then turns to all the disciples and says, "If any of you wants to be my follower, you must give up your own way, take up your cross, and follow me. If you try to hang on to your life, you will lose it. But if you give up your life for my sake, you will save it" (Matthew 16:24-25, NLT). Jesus is telling the disciples—and us—that moving beyond our distorted attachment defaults and insecure survival strategies will feel like dying. It will feel like carrying our own cross around, a cross "through which the world has been crucified to me, and I to the world," as the apostle Paul says (Galatians 6:14). Jesus is inviting us to die with him.

The unfortunate reality is that sometimes when we think we are learning to carry our cross, we are just exchanging one insecure image of God for a different one. As a person in one of our trainings said, "At one point in my life I just traded the Jungle for the Desert. I just ran to the other side of the cage and proclaimed myself free." But trading images of God is not the same thing as becoming deeply attached to God.

The Pain of Coming Undone

Like an attuned caregiver, Jesus is willing to meet us when we come to the end of ourselves, when our attachment strategies no longer work. He meets us right where we are. He sees our weakness. He knows our insecurities. He understands how our nervous systems were shaped and formed by our insecure attachments. He knows the defaults we live from better than we know them ourselves. And he comes to us with compassion and curiosity rather than condemnation and criticism.

Early in our faith, Jesus might meet a Jungle dweller in a non-verbal emotional encounter or through a deep moment of love and affirmation. Jesus might meet a Desert dweller in a very cognitive way, through the logic of salvation when they've come to the end of their rope. Jesus might meet a War Zone dweller in either or even both of these ways. The ways we first become aware of God's presence are often familiar attachment pathways. How else could God meet us? Jesus knows what we need to recognize him as our loving and attuned attachment figure—even if that means meeting us in a way that fits our current insecurities, attachment strategies, and distorted defaults.

But like Jesus resisting Peter's attempts to drag him into his insecure attachment, Jesus refuses to become a Jungle, Desert, or War Zone god. If we continue trying to drag Jesus into our implicit attachment defaults, we will find ourselves frustrated and confused. Eventually, all our attempts to make Jesus be who we want him to be will fail.

When this happens, our early ways of relating to Jesus might not work as well anymore. Jesus is shaking up our attachment defaults by drawing us out of our old survival strategies. For a Jungle dweller, this could mean your emotional experiences dry up. Jesus might be moving you to use more cognitive tools to connect with him in patterns and truth. It might also look like a Desert dweller finding a place of confusion where faith isn't making sense like it used to. These experiences can be highly disturbing—especially if you find yourself in a faith community that doesn't have language to help you understand what is happening.

When Jesus moves you in these ways, it will feel a little bit like death. It will feel like the dying of faith, even of your sense of self. What used to feel like faith turns to fear. What used to be hope turns to despair. You become confused about how to keep loving God when it doesn't seem that God is loving you.

This is when it's tempting to do what Luke and Hannah did. It's tempting to drag Jesus into your landscape so that you won't have to face dying to yourself, letting go of your well-practiced survival strategies. You can deconstruct faith, and that cognitive dissonance will feel like dying. You can leave a faith community, and that social displacement will feel like dying. It is possible that you should put off a shallow version of Christianity or leave an unhealthy church. But that isn't the kind of dying Jesus is talking about. Because in doing those things, you might just be finding a way to fit God into your insecure attachments, which won't bring the healing you so desperately want. It won't set you free the way you think it will.

What if, instead, you could receive the invitation to die to yourself as the invitation to see Jesus for who he really is? What if this feeling of hitting a wall or walking through a dark night is actually an invitation to recognize that you are still moving toward the Pasture of secure attachment? You don't really know Jesus like you thought you did. Maybe those disappointments are showing you where you tried to drag Jesus into your insecure landscape.

Old and New Self

The New Testament names this as the struggle between the old self and the new self, a struggle happening in our minds and our bodies.

Paul urges us to put off the old self and to put on the new self in Christ. To the church in Ephesus, he writes, "You were taught, with regard to your former way of life, to put off your old self, which is being corrupted by its deceitful desires; to be made new in the attitude of your minds; and to put on the new self, created to be like God in true righteousness and holiness" (Ephesians 4:22-24). In the letter to the Colossians, he urges them to stop sinning, "since you have taken off your old self with its practices and have put on the new self, which is being renewed in knowledge in the image of its Creator"

(Colossians 3:9-10). And as he reminds those in Corinth, "If anyone is in Christ, the new creation has come: The old has gone, the new is here!" (2 Corinthians 5:17).

But Paul desperately knows the struggle of living as this new creation, as this new self. The old self, or sinful nature, with its survival strategies that lead us to sin, is always ready to jump in. Paul says that when he wants to do what is right and good, he can't. And when he doesn't want to do what is wrong, the impulse is right there and he does it anyway. He says sin is living inside him (see Romans 7:18-20). This is what happens to Peter when he rebukes Jesus. His survival strategies take over and he acts from sinful protection.

The Good Shepherd meets us in our old lives but invites us to move toward the Pasture of joyful connection and secure attachment. At some point—call it hitting the wall, the dark night of the soul, or passing through the valley of the shadow of death—the Good Shepherd's movement in our lives will feel like death. But he allows this so that we might dwell in the house of the Lord forever. Moving from the landscapes in which we find ourselves to the Pasture requires us to pass through death. This death to our survival strategies opens up a life that is the deepening of our attachment with God.

This dying that opens to a deeper life is something we can long for and ask for, but ultimately it's something only Jesus can do for us. We have to place our faith in him, even if it is just a little. We can say with the father who brought his son to Jesus for healing, "I believe; help my unbelief!" (Mark 9:24, NRSV).

If you truly want to release your understanding of Jesus as the Jungle, Desert, or War Zone god you have implicitly believed him to be, you must surrender yourself to your own undoing, die with Jesus, and rise to life in the Pasture with the Good Shepherd.

Consolation and Desolation

For hundreds of years, people have practiced looking back at their days through the lens of *consolation* and *desolation* in their practice of the Examen. Anything that builds or draws you into deeper faith, hope, or love is *consolation*. It's a movement toward God. The opposite is *desolation*, anything that feels like movement away from God or that brings a decrease in faith, hope, or love. Consolation is received as a gift or grace from God, something we can't earn but can only receive. Desolation is understood to be temporary. Just as the sun rises after the darkness of night, so desolation doesn't last forever.

Without going into great depth here, desolation and consolation work differently, depending on whether you intend to faithfully follow Jesus. When you are serious about following Jesus, you will find consolation when you are moving toward obedience and faithfulness, and desolation when you are moving away. This is the work of the Holy Spirit to keep you close.

However, when you are generally uninterested or consciously choosing not to follow Jesus, you will find consolation in things that continue to lead you further away from Jesus and desolation in things that could potentially bring you closer. This is the testing of the enemy, trying to keep you from returning to joy and attaching securely to God.

Because of this tricky dynamic, deconstructing your *faith* has the potential to be a process that leads you further away from God rather than closer. However, deconstructing your *attachment strategies* (your awareness of God and your practice of faith) has the potential to bring you much closer to God. The difference comes in your intention. If you intend to stay close to Jesus, your desolation and consolation will help you discern what is bringing you an increase in faith, hope, and love. If you are not committed to following Jesus but are instead committed to feeling better about your faith—whether you end up trusting Jesus or not—there's a good chance your consolation and desolation may be misguided.[3]

We hope and pray that you can see that your attachment strategies may have caused your misunderstandings of God, rather than God being the problem. We hope you remain committed to learning to trust Jesus as he truly is rather than as you've seen him through your defaults.

Practice: Examen of Consolation and Desolation

- *Begin by taking a couple of deep breaths—in through your nose and out through your mouth. As you do this, remember God's gladness to be with you, no matter how you come into this time. Ask the Holy Spirit to help you notice what you need to notice.*
- *Next, affirm your desire to trust Jesus as he truly is and surrendering to the possibility that some of your attachment defaults need to be rewritten.*
- *Recall your day in the order in which it happened, with an eye toward finding the good things. Especially notice any places where you experienced consolation: an increase of faith, hope, or love.*
- *Now thank God for these things. Appreciate them as specific gifts, expressions of God's provision and availability to you.*
- *Now review the day again, noticing any places where you experienced desolation.* ***Where did I notice a decrease in or resistance toward faith, hope, or love? Where am I feeling the pull of my old self? Where am I uncertain that I am seeing Jesus as he is and not the way I've dragged him into my landscape? Where was I frustrated in my faith today? What might my frustration reveal about my attachment? Where might I need to die to my old self?***
- *Talk with Jesus about what you discover.* ***What does Jesus celebrate with me? What does he grieve with me? Where did I experience ruptures—with Jesus, with other people, with my new self? Is there anything I need to do to make repairs?***
- *Ask him for what you want:* ***to recognize old attachment strategies (my old self) influencing me, to surrender to dying to the old so that Jesus can raise me into the new, wisdom in knowing how to position myself to make more room for the Holy Spirit to reveal more of my new self, other people I can talk to about these things.***
- *Think about what you know about your day tomorrow. Reaffirm your desire to trust Jesus as your new attachment figure. What do you want to ask Jesus for?*

CHAPTER 13

LIVING WITH JESUS: LOVING GOD, LOVING OTHERS

Perhaps the most surprising thing about following Jesus is how what looks like death almost always produces life beyond our wildest imaginings. The disciples despaired after the crucifixion but were shocked and elated when Jesus rose again. They were heartbroken when Jesus ascended to heaven but were empowered beyond belief when the Holy Spirit filled them on Pentecost. Like the disciples, what feels like death can be the beginning of a fuller, deeper life than we could have imagined.

When we surrender to the painful undoing of our attachment strategies and are willing to release our insecure expectations of God, we can return to God's good design for us: joyful connection, intimacy and independence, and a *yes* attachment default. Spiritual writers throughout the ages have spoken of this as letting go of the false self in order to become our true self. While popularization of this language hasn't always done the tradition justice, Albert Haase uses something close to attachment language when he defines the true self:

> With childlike simplicity and spontaneity, the true self is dependent and has a relationship with thee (others) in the

> here and now as the sacred place of encounter with Thee (God). . . . We need to return to being who God created us to be and stop being who we are not. We need to come back home to the true self. . . . The great tragedy for many of us is that in growing up, we become self-made, independent successes who are weighed down by thoughts of the past and worries about the future. We lose touch with our true self, the person God created us to be. We live off-center and alienated from who we really are.[1]

Through our insecure attachment strategies, we have cobbled together a self that is shaped by our early survival. It is good to survive in a sinful world, but our survival strategies will be marked by that sin. We have formed defaults that define how we see others, God, the world, and ourselves. These defaults got us to where we are because they helped us survive to see this day. But tragically, they are not true. And because we are attached in insecure ways, we are not truly free. Instead we are hindered in our ability to live in faith, hope, and love.

These sinful survival strategies infect the way we pray, read the Bible, participate in worship, and especially engage in Christian community. We turn to prayer, the Bible, worship, or community for encouragement and growth, but instead we find discouragement and stagnation.

We see the world through our own attachment strategies. What one person calls safe, another calls a threat. Where one person sees connection, someone else feels the need to protect. As we saw in the landscape chapters, we all approach God, and consequently our faith and church communities, from particular defaults. Those defaults are at play every time we approach God in prayer, sit down to read the Bible, set foot in a worship service, or participate in Christian community. If we approach this reality from the thrival skill of mutual responsibility for fault, we can see that it's not always our fault. Nor is it the fault of the church we're attending, the small group leader we're frustrated with, or the Bible translation we're reading. It's not God's fault either. We see everything through a particular attachment lens, and it's time to change our glasses.

But we can't change our attachment on our own. Jesus, as our attachment figure, is the one who offers attachment to us. Jesus offers joyful connection and opportunities to grow in intimacy and independence. Our Good Shepherd is always available to alleviate our distress and to activate our agency. He repairs our ruptures. And Jesus is the only one who can increase our faith, expand our hope, and deepen our love. But we are not entirely passive in the process. We participate in the work of God to secure our attachment by purposefully placing ourselves in the way of God's grace. We open ourselves to what God is doing, train ourselves to attend to God's activity, and respond to the initiative God is taking in our lives.

And so we come now to spiritual disciplines—practices that help us participate in God's desire to rewrite our attachment defaults and move us into the Pasture.

Jesus Meets Us and Moves Us

As you read through this chapter, remember that Jesus both meets you in what is comfortable *and* moves you into discomfort toward the Pasture. You don't secure your attachment to God simply by reading a book. Your nervous system was shaped and your strategies became comfortable with practice, over time, in relationship with people. In order to shift your attachment, you will need time, patience, practice, and people.

We recommend that you choose some "meeting" practices to bring you encouragement and hope as well as at least one "moving" practice to begin responding to Jesus' invitation to move toward the Pasture. Don't choose all "moving" practices, or you will become frustrated and probably want to give up entirely. Instead, celebrate the practices that allow you to feel met by Jesus while also stretching toward moving.

Moving practices can feel uncomfortable and challenging. Meeting practices can feel good but may not produce much fruit. So how can we know which practices to keep up with? As a way of discerning what to do, we encourage you to frame your practices according to what Ignatius of Loyola called *consolation* and *desolation* (see pages 187–188). Anything that builds or draws you into deeper faith, hope, or love is consolation. It's a movement toward God. The opposite is desolation, anything that feels like a movement away from God or that brings a decrease in faith, hope, or love. Consolation is received as a gift or grace from God, something we can't earn but can only receive. Desolation is understood to be temporary—it doesn't last forever. When you understand that times of desolation are normal, it becomes less disturbing to experience them. You don't need to rush to fix them. In fact, Ignatius recommended that you continue to practice what you decided to practice while you were in consolation rather than changing or giving up in the face of the desolation.

So as you engage these practices, we encourage you to continue the Examen as a metapractice to keep you in touch with the overall direction of your faith, hope, and love. Ask yourself, *As I engage each new practice, how do I see its potential to contribute to an increase in faith, hope, or love over time?* Also recall the importance of recommitting each day to trusting Jesus as your new attachment figure, even when that means he might need to move you away from what's comfortable into places that feel uncomfortable. He is your Good Shepherd, even in the valley of the shadow of death.

Note that although we will speak about prayer and Bible reading as individual practices, these are also great communal practices. Any of the things we suggest as individual practices can be shared with small groups of people. You'll also notice that we included worship and community as categories of practice. Remember, you didn't get where you are by yourself. You won't change by yourself. If your true self is shaped by relationships in the present with others *and* with God, you need to have interactions with both.

A special note to our War Zone readers: Remember that while we do not specifically address your frustrations or which of these practices might be meeting or moving for you, you might find resonance with both Jungle and Desert strategies and practices. Try practicing any and all of the disciplines we suggest, and notice how they affect you.

Prayer

Praying Toward the Pasture

James (from the Desert chapter) prayed in the morning using structures he had been taught. James's prayers were rarely specific or personal, revolving around tasks and events more than people. God felt distant to James as he prayed. But he knew prayer was important, so he prayed daily for God to help him to be obedient and faithful.

Abigail (from the Jungle chapter) had a feeling that she had to earn God's listening ear, even though she wouldn't say it out loud. If she felt disconnected from God, it confirmed her anxiety that she wasn't doing it right. Sometimes Abigail felt like her prayers were getting through and God was hearing her. But when she didn't feel God's presence or see answers, she either doubled down and prayed even more exuberantly or would gradually stop praying for days or weeks without realizing it.

Thankfully, Jesus meets us where we are in prayer. He also invites us to move deeper into the Pasture.

After learning about attachment and recognizing his location in the Desert, James felt invited to pray more relational prayers. He would start his prayer time by focusing on the Aaronic blessing, allowing himself to receive God's face shining upon him (see Numbers 6:22-27). When he found that his mind was wandering from his prayer, he gave himself permission to pray through whatever was on his mind, even if that meant leaving the structure he was accustomed to. He began to shift the focus of prayer from tasks to relationships. He now prays for the grace to grow in his own attachment and for compassion to understand others. In general, he still uses a structure to pray, but his prayers have become more specific and more personal as he stretches toward believing that Jesus cares about him as a person.

Abigail, once she discovered she was living in the Jungle, started to remind herself that she was always accepted and deeply loved, no matter how she felt. She reminded herself that whether she felt it or not, God wanted her to know the path of life and fullness of joy (see Psalm 16:11). She practiced being quiet before the Lord and enjoying his presence. Before she prays, she remembers the feeling of walking into a room and having a friend be genuinely glad to see her. She imagines the gaze of Jesus, glad to see her coming in prayer. Imagining Jesus' gladness draws her into remembering times of joy and connection with God. These practices are helping to build her trust in the consistent availability of Jesus. Her *maybe* is shifting to a *yes*.

Practicing Pasture Prayers

No matter which attachment landscape you find yourself in and how you might be praying, we would like to offer you a couple of prayer practices. Both will meet and move you in different ways depending on your landscape but can draw you deeper into the Pasture to live a resurrection life with the Good Shepherd.

RETURNING TO JOY BEFORE PRAYING

Both James and Abigail have adopted a practice of returning to joyful connection before they pray. James remembers that God's face is shining upon him, and Abigail recalls Jesus' gladness to be with her. The reason God can feel so distant in prayer is that without realizing it, we are praying from a posture of protection rather than connection. Connecting to joy before or through prayer builds the thrival skill of integrated processing. By focusing the mind on what is true about God, you are strengthening your cognitive-linear processing. But by focusing on God's joy or delight or love toward you, you are stretching your social-emotional processing. And doing this will calm your nervous system before talking with God, shifting you from protection to connection.

PERSONALIZED PRAYER STRUCTURE: PSALM 23

Like the Lord's Prayer, Psalm 23 can be used as a personalized prayer structure. The first verse of Psalm 23 is a thesis statement for being deeply attached to God: "The LORD is my shepherd; I have all that I need" (NLT). For our purposes, this can be translated as *Because Jesus is my attachment figure, I trust that he is available, that my distress will be alleviated, and that I can use my agency for the good of the world. I am okay. I lack nothing.*

Declaring words of trust like this can shape us over time.

From this declaration of security, we can allow each statement of Psalm 23 (NLT) to form our prayers:

- "He lets me rest in green meadows; he leads me beside peaceful streams." *How is Jesus inviting me to rest? How is he providing for my most basic needs?*
- "He renews my strength." *How and where do I need his strength?*
- "He guides me along right paths, bringing honor to his name." *Where do I need his wisdom and guidance? How can I live in a way that makes others curious about the Good Shepherd?*
- "Even when I walk through the darkest valley, I will not be afraid, for you are close beside me." *What are the dark valleys in my life? How do I need Jesus to walk with me there?*
- "Your rod and your staff protect and comfort me." *Where do I need protection? Comfort?*
- "You prepare a feast for me in the presence of my enemies." *How is Jesus taking care of me even when I feel attacked or opposed?*
- "You honor me by anointing my head with oil. My cup overflows with blessings." *What are the gifts I can thank God for?*
- "Surely your goodness and unfailing love will pursue me all the days of my life, and I will live in the house of the LORD forever." *Where can I recognize God's goodness and love today? How can I remind myself that I live in the house of the Lord already—that I belong and have a place in God's house?*

If you find yourself in the Desert, the challenge of this kind of prayer structure is the personalizing part (pursuing intimacy through social-emotional processing). Getting specific about your inner life, as well as your external circumstances, helps you to see that God cares about all of you. God doesn't care only about your finances or your success at work but also about your depressive thoughts, your anger, and your anxiety.

If you find yourself in the Jungle, it is the structure that will challenge you (practicing independence through logical-linear format). Without a structure, you might not push yourself to focus on the good things in your life and on God's presence with you, even in the dark places. A structure helps you get outside your social-emotional processes (which can tend toward negative rumination). It helps you spend more time remembering who God is and how your Good Shepherd is already tending to you.

Silence and Solitude

We saw earlier how Jesus engaged in silence and solitude early in the morning as a practice of intimacy. He did this alongside his movement outward of independence in mission. While chronic loneliness is mentally and spiritually detrimental, the ability to be alone with God and with ourselves moves us toward maturity.[2]

Both Desert and Jungle dwellers will resist silence and solitude, but for different reasons.

Jungle dwellers might initially like the idea of silence and solitude because they never get any. Their life is so full of relational noise that the idea of a break sounds amazing. But once they enter into silence and solitude, two things might happen. First, they might find they actually hate being alone. A Jungle dweller's brain and body is shaped to seek intimacy with others. So being alone automatically produces anxiety. Second, this anxiety is compounded because, within the silence, deeper feelings of fear, regret, and shame emerge, along with the deeper realization that you aren't sure who you are without your people. But because you are all alone, you don't have anyone to help you coregulate these buried emotions.

This is where Jesus meets and moves a Jungle dweller. Jesus will *meet* you in the silence and solitude and remind you that you are not alone. He is with you. And over time he will *move* you toward a deeper attachment with him as he helps you coregulate your emotions, your distress, your guilt, and your shame. Through the practice of silence and solitude, you begin to learn that Jesus is the person you can go to. He is "your people."

Desert dwellers might also like the idea of silence and solitude, but not because of any inherent spiritual maturity. You just like to be alone, so it is easy to believe you are more advanced in this discipline than you really are. But once you start practicing silence and solitude, you will quickly tire of it for two reasons. First, it is not productive. Nothing is happening. Because Desert dwellers focus on agency and independence, they like to see results. But there is no action and there are no results in silence and solitude. Second, and even worse, silence and solitude will likely open you up to the deeper feelings and emotions you are trying to avoid.

Like the Jungle dweller, this is where Jesus meets and moves the person in the Desert. Jesus will *meet* you in silence and solitude by affirming that your deepest longing for connection cannot be truly met by other people. But Jesus will *move* you toward deep attachment with God by offering you deep connection without rejection, deep community without abandonment. And Jesus will remind you that life is not all about how productive and active you are. In silence and solitude, Jesus will move you toward integrating your independence with a new sense of intimacy.

Immanuel Journaling

Throughout the book we have talked about how attuned parents foster secure attachment. Parents are attuned when they see, hear, and understand their children. Immanuel journaling is a way to receive the attunement of Jesus, our Good Shepherd. Jesus knows how we experience the world, and receiving his attunement helps us to feel seen, known, and understood.[3]

Here's how you can practice Immanuel journaling:

- Begin with a specific gratitude to God (anything in that moment, from the last day or week, or anything from your life). (For example, *Jesus, thank you for the birdsong this morning following the rain. It reminds me that storms don't last forever and that joy returns in the morning.*)
- Following your expression of gratitude, imagine how Jesus might respond to you. When you thank a person in your life, they are bound to have some kind of reaction. How does Jesus respond to you thanking him?
- Now allow yourself to imagine Jesus talking with you as he would with one of his disciples in the Gospels. Writing in the first person, from the perspective of Jesus, let Jesus attune to you using phrases beginning with "I see you," "I hear you," "I understand," "I'm glad to be with you," and "I'm doing something." When you write these words in God's voice, they might look something like this:
    - "I see you, sitting in your favorite chair, holding your coffee and wearing your pajamas."

  - "I hear you worrying about the meeting you have today. You're feeling unprepared and nervous."
  - "I understand how much this means to you. I understand why you're feeling anxious about this."
  - "I'm glad to be with you right now and in the meeting later today. No matter how the meeting goes, I am glad to be with you."
  - "I can give you wisdom and strength. Remember that I am generous and will give you wisdom when you ask for it. I'll be with you in the meeting. Find my face, and stay connected with me."

- Finally, read what you've written out loud. This allows the words to sink in more deeply. Even better, read what you've written to someone you trust. This is sharing your joyful connection and Jesus' attunement with another person. If you both experience peace as you read what you wrote, you can feel more sure that this is something Jesus would say to someone he loves. This builds your connection not only with Jesus but also with another person.

If you find yourself in the Desert, this will be a *moving* practice for you. It may feel like breaking a rule to write in God's voice. As a check, we always test what we write with the question, "Does this sound like something Jesus would say to someone he loves? Does it align with what we know about Jesus from the Bible?" We have noticed the pattern that the "I am doing something" section at the end is often saturated with Scripture. Even in the example above, you see an echo of James 1:5: "If any of you lacks wisdom, you should ask God, who gives generously to all without finding fault, and it will be given to you." Reading what you've written out loud to someone else might feel like way too much for you, but maybe consider sharing this practice with another Desert dweller.

If you find yourself in the Jungle, this will be a *meeting* practice for you, connecting to your desire to be seen, heard, and known. It might feel appealing for you to read it aloud to another person as well. Or it could be terrifying. Either way, it's a great way to build connections with people and with Jesus. It can become a *moving* practice for you in your relationships with people. When you feel desperate to connect with and be understood by other people in your life, shift that desire to Jesus through Immanuel journaling. Once you've received attunement from Jesus, your need to be understood by the person will decrease and you'll be able to enter into conversation with that person from a place of connection rather than protection. Jesus meets us in the desire for joyful connection and moves us toward finding the depths of that connection in himself—the Good Shepherd who came to give us fullness of life (see John 10:10).

Bible Reading

Reading the Bible from Different Landscapes

Every morning, James sat down with his study Bible, focusing on a single book at a time, following the cross-references to other parts of the Bible. He liked knowing the historical context behind what he was reading and often read with commentaries. He rarely felt like the Bible was speaking specifically to him in the present. It was more like he was observing how God had dealt with his people in the past.

Abigail focused on short devotional snippets of Scripture, largely dedicated to making life work. She started book studies but rarely finished them, instead reading her favorite stories and psalms over and over again. There were large parts of the Bible that Abigail skipped over or avoided. She didn't know what to do with the God who was portrayed in some of the Old Testament narratives, and she didn't like some of Paul's harshness to the early churches. She stuck with what was comforting to her.

After James recognized he lived from the Desert and started seeing Jesus as his new attachment figure, he saw relational neuroscience all over the Bible! He noticed the themes of joy, God's face, rupture and repair, and God's availability to his people and sending them out with agency. He was struck by how relational Jesus is in the Gospels. He spent time imagining himself in the stories as one of the disciples, noticing how he reacted to Jesus. The Bible, which he used to read strictly for information, came alive for him in new ways. As in prayer, James was growing the thrival skill of integrated processing by joining the logical-linear nature of God's written Word to the social-emotional content within the Bible.

Rather than reading the Bible to find a word to comfort her in the present, Abigail pushed herself to read the parts of the Bible she used to skip. She wanted to see how the whole Bible tells the story of a God who longs to be known and in relationship with his people. As she learned the history of early Israel and the surrounding nations, she saw the rules of the Old Testament as merciful rather than oppressive. She now enjoys studying more deeply, looking for literary patterns and imagery, as well as appreciating the rigorous logic Paul used.

Practicing Pasture Reading

No matter which landscape you find yourself in and how you might be engaging with the Bible, we would like to offer you a few practices. With each one, Jesus will meet and move you in different ways depending on your attachment landscape. But no matter your attachment strategies, all of these will draw you deeper into the Pasture.

IMMANUEL JOURNALING WITH THE BIBLE

As described above, Immanuel journaling is a way of receiving attunement from Jesus. You can also use Immanuel journaling within your practice of Bible reading. As you read a part of Scripture, notice how it is affecting you and let Jesus attune to you, talking specifically about how you're experiencing what you just read.

If you find yourself in the Desert, Jesus will *meet* you through your desire to engage deeply in Scripture. But he will also invite you to *move* into the Pasture, shifting you from looking at the information to engaging with him through the Bible. Jesus cares how you respond to his words, even welcoming you amid your doubts and questions. He doesn't just want you to read; he wants to be with you as you read.

If you find yourself in the Jungle, Jesus will *meet* you by giving you permission to feel your emotions as you read. But he will also invite you to *move* into the Pasture as you tackle parts of the Bible you used to avoid. Jesus can handle your discomfort. You can bring even the tough parts to him.[4]

IMAGINATIVE READING

Reading with your imagination allows you to interact with a biblical narrative as if you were there. When you fill out the details of the scene with your imagination, you are using logical-linear processes to place yourself in the story. When you ask what people are feeling and why they are doing what they are doing, you are using social-emotional processing to dig deeper into the narrative. Exercising these will grow your thrival skill of integrated processing, connecting logical-linear and social-emotional aspects within your practice of reading the Bible.

Think about some of the questions you might ask if you were reading the narrative of Jesus healing Bartimaeus's blindness (see Mark 10:46-52):

- What would it be like to be one of the people on the road near the city gates?
- What would you see from where you stood?
- What might you hear in the crowd?
- What might you smell? Or taste?
- What would Bartimaeus's voice sound like? What about the people who tried to silence him?
- What would you feel as you were surrounded by people and listened to the desperation in Bartimaeus's voice?
- What would you experience as Jesus called Bartimaeus to come and then asked him what he wanted?
- How would you react to witnessing a man you've known was blind now saying he can see?
- What questions might you have for Jesus?

Allow what you imagine to become a springboard for conversation with Jesus. You might even want to use Immanuel journaling to allow Jesus to attune to your imaginative experience of this encounter.

For a Desert dweller, this might sound like nonsense. Why would you imagine what's not explicitly detailed in Scripture? Isn't that making things up and adding to God's Word? Allow Jesus to *meet* you in your high value for God's Word and give it a try anyway. Being lopsided toward logical-linear processing, it is possible you are missing or distorting aspects of God's Word. Strengthening your social-emotional processing might actually deepen your access to the truth that has always been there. Allow Jesus to *move* you into a fuller experience of these stories as you imagine what it might have been like for real, flesh-and-blood people to experience his presence in such a concrete and tangible way. If this is hard for you, consider inviting a Jungle dweller to imagine the same Scripture and then have a conversation about what you both experienced.

From the Jungle, you might feel excited about this idea. Because it's not a stretch for you to imagine how people in the narrative might be experiencing it, it's easier for you to put yourself in the midst of the story. Jesus will *meet* you in this way, enjoying and celebrating your strength. The invitation to *move* deeper into the Pasture is to test whether your imagination is just confirming aspects of your insecure attachment history (dragging Jesus into your landscape), or whether you are being transformed into deep faith, hope, and love (Jesus drawing you into the Pasture). Consider sharing your experience with someone in the Desert to see how their logical-linear thinking might inform your imaginary experience.

LECTIO DIVINA

The ancient practice of lectio divina is a slow, reflective way of reading Scripture. Unlike imaginative reading, which strengthens your agency through imagination, lectio divina is a surrender of agency as you move toward intimacy with God, allowing the Holy Spirit to focus your attention on a part of Scripture. We suggest you follow these steps:

- Return to joy (see page 196).
- Ask Jesus, with the Holy Spirit, to read with you, giving you understanding and insight. Ask the Spirit to direct your focus.
- *Read* a small segment of the Bible, slowly and prayerfully. Reread the segment a few times, possibly emphasizing different words, taking pauses at different times. Notice what stands out to you. This is what the Spirit is bringing forward for you. Think of the verses as a meal, chewing each bite slowly.[5]
- *Reflect* on what you've read. Repeat any words or phrases that have caught your attention. Be curious about how this word might be personal for you today. Allow the word to interact with your thoughts, emotions, desires, and your attachment history.

- *Respond* in conversation with Jesus, your attachment figure. He meets you where you are and attunes to you and your reflection on what you've read. What do you want to talk with him about in response to reading this? You may choose to do some Immanuel journaling at this point.
- *Rest* in what you've received. It's okay to just be with Jesus. You don't need to talk. Just rest with him. You don't need to make anything happen, and what you experience doesn't need to be profound. Just sit in his presence, enjoying his face turned toward you.

Desert dwellers might find this to be a *meeting* practice because it allows you to remain rooted in the Bible. However, it might also be a *moving* practice because it brings your reading into your personal life through attunement with Jesus. As you notice your thoughts, emotions, and desires and how they intersect with the words you're reading, you are opening yourself to new levels of intimacy with Jesus.

Jungle dwellers might also find this to be a *meeting* practice because it allows you to connect with Jesus in an intimate way. It might also be a *moving* practice in that you need to slow down and read a few times, really paying attention to the words.

BIBLICAL STUDY

Digging into the historical context of the Bible can deepen our understanding of what it means for us today. Just as Abigail was able to see God's mercy in the Old Testament compared to ancient gods, so we can see how good God is when we understand more about the times in which the Bible was written. Utilizing a great commentary series or an app like Read Scripture from the Bible Project, you can gain insight into how the original audiences might have read each part of Scripture.

This is a *meeting* practice for Desert dwellers, who already appreciate studying. Enjoy and celebrate your strength in logical-linear reasoning and your ability to look at the details. As a *moving* practice, you might spend more time in the wisdom and poetry writings of Job, Psalms, Proverbs, Ecclesiastes, and Song of Songs, especially focusing on the emotions expressed in these passages.

This is a *moving* practice for Jungle dwellers. Studying might not be your natural way to engage with Scripture, but understanding the bigger picture in which the Bible is set will expand your ability to allow what you read to connect with your life in a more meaningful way.

Corporate Worship: Local Church

Corporate Worship from Different Landscapes

James enjoyed his church. It was Desert friendly. The service included kneeling and standing and gave him words to pray in the liturgy, and he appreciated the minimalistic worship team. The hymns were theologically sound, and he appreciated the way doctrine was threaded throughout the service. The preaching was solid, and he learned a lot every week. He loved that his church didn't do a meet-and-greet time.

But James knew he needed a community of people to run new attachment experiments with and stumbled on a charismatic liturgical church. Before moving deeper into the Pasture of secure attachment, James would have thought their style of worship was too exuberant, minimized the sermon, and emphasized communion too much. But now he is finding that both the people and the service align with where Jesus is moving him. This community gives space for more expressive singing and praying, and James finds that the combination of the liturgy he loves with the new emphasis on life in the Spirit is a great way for him to practice intimacy and independence within community.

Abigail loved the times of musical worship at her church. She was glad to learn during the sermon, but it was the singing that kept her coming back. She liked the freedom to sway and kneel if she wanted to. But she often worried whether she was "feeling it" as much as others around her. Then she might sing even louder or more expressively. The comparison and inner criticism sometimes disrupted her ability to worship altogether.

As Abigail is growing in her attachment with Jesus, she is less concerned about how she measures up to the people worshiping around her. She is still glad to worship alongside others, but now she finds it to be delightful rather than discouraging. She is becoming more connected with the communal reading of Scripture and engaging with the sermons by paying attention to the main ideas as well as how she responds to what she hears. She is embracing the communion liturgy and finding richness in the tradition of it, rather than struggling with the rote feeling of it.

Practicing Pasture Worship

CONFESSION

A long-standing practice in corporate worship, confession helps us all to recognize that none of us deserve the attachment love of God. It puts all of us on equal footing. Jungle dwellers might get stuck heaping shame upon themselves in confession because you are already prone to believe it's all your fault. Desert dwellers might skim over the surface of confession rather than allowing yourself to engage in any kind of specific or personal way. But confession, at its core, is a recognition of reality. None of us are capable of living in the Pasture without the Good Shepherd. This is common ground for all landscapes. When we confess, corporately, that we are in need of God's attachment love and grace, we find that none of us are alone. No one is further ahead or better. There is no comparison. All of us stand together in our need for the Good Shepherd.

If you're not currently worshiping in a community that practices corporate confession, you might consider gathering a small group of people you trust to start practicing confession with. You might begin by praying the prayer of confession from *The Book of Common Prayer* together:

> Most merciful God, we confess that we have sinned against you in thought, word, and deed, by what we have done, and by what we have left undone. We have not loved you with our whole heart; we have not loved our neighbors as ourselves. We are truly sorry and we humbly repent. For the sake of your Son Jesus Christ, have mercy on us and forgive us; that we may delight in your will, and walk in your ways, to the glory of your Name. Amen.

If you begin this way, you don't need to be specific or personal but just acknowledge that you all start from the same place. As trust develops within the group, perhaps you can leave time between phrases of the prayer for people to confess specific things. Whatever you do, be sure to always offer assurance of forgiveness after the confession (for example, the words from 1 John 1:9).

USING YOUR BODY

Paul urges us to "give your bodies to God because of all he has done for you. Let them be a living and holy sacrifice—the kind he will find acceptable. This is truly the way to worship him" (Romans 12:1, NLT). This is a call to be mindful about what we do with our bodies, including how we bodily participate in worship. There's much more to say on this topic, but for our purposes here, we want to unite our mind, body, and emotions toward the thrival skill of integrated processing.

Being intentional about how you worship with your body is important for both Desert and Jungle dwellers. Depending on the nature of the worship settings you're in, there might be opportunities to kneel, stand, sing, speak aloud in a communal reading, or move your body in other ways. You can also notice the bodies around you. There is something profound about gathering together as God's people, coming together as a local expression of the body of Christ.

Asking yourself a few questions about how your body is involved in worship can help you integrate your mind, heart, and body in worship:

- *How can I physically express my appreciation and affection for God?* Lifting hands, placing your hands over your heart, and even smiling are ways to let your appreciation show in an embodied way.
- *How can I train my internal world by moving my body?* Kneeling, opening your hands, bowing your head, or singing can be ways to move yourself into postures and shapes that train your mind and heart to engage in new ways.
- *How can I be aware of other bodies around me? How can the movements of others contribute to our corporate worship? How do I move in ways that help others around me enter into worship?*

TAKING NOTES

You might already take notes during the sermon, but what if you started noticing different things? As you write down the main ideas or phrases that stand out to you, try also noticing how you respond to what is being said.

- Where do you see God offering joyful connection? Intimacy? Independence? Availability? Alleviation of distress? Agency to love?
- What brings you peace and joy? Where do you feel challenged?

- What do you hear about Jesus as your attachment figure?
- What are you distracted by? What might these distractions tell you?

To make this a communal practice, share your observations with someone after the worship service (and listen to theirs as well). This would be especially interesting to do with someone in a different landscape from you as you both seek to move toward the Pasture.

COMMUNION

Like confession, sharing communion together puts us all on common ground. The Lord's Supper is an integration of past, present, and future as well as an integration of body, soul, and mind.

Together we remember the night on which Jesus was betrayed and ate the Passover meal with his disciples. We remember that he surrendered his body to death and offered a new covenant in his shed blood. In the present, we gather as individual members of the body of Christ in a local community. We surrender ourselves in obedience to Christ and share his life together with our brothers and sisters. Together we anticipate the future wedding feast of the Lamb, when Jesus will share this feast with us for all eternity. Remembering the past, receiving the elements in the present, and anticipating the future all engage our minds.

As we touch the bread, taste the juice or wine, and chew and swallow, we take the new life of Christ into our bodies, digesting his generosity and mercy. Many churches recite words together and stand, sit, and move around the space to come to the table. These movements allow us to offer our bodies to Jesus and to mingle with other bodies around us. As we practice this communal participation in the life of Jesus, we are integrating mind, body, and soul.

If your worshiping community doesn't currently practice communion together on a regular basis, we encourage you to start collecting a smaller group of people to share this practice with. In the early church, communion was likely a shared meal with the remembrance of Christ at the center. Invite some friends over for a meal and read one of the Scripture passages that contains the words of institution of the Lord's Supper (see Matthew 26:17-29; Mark 14:12-25; Luke 22:7-38; 1 Corinthians 11:23-25), and then eat together, sharing your lives and encouraging one another in your faith.

Christian Community

Participating in Community from Different Landscapes

James knew he should participate in community. He was comfortable gathering with people for a clear purpose: a service project, helping someone move, unloading the food pantry delivery, playing a soccer game, and so on. At potlucks and picnics, James was glad to help set up or move tables—anything so he didn't have to just stand around and make small talk. He went to a small group with his wife, learned the "rules" of the group, and had a surface-level connection with the people. But he dreaded having to go every week. He neither felt deeply known by others nor had the desire to know others more deeply. He was better at getting things done together.

As he began to stretch himself, he decided to organize a group of guys around a book he wanted to read. Sure, it was a nonfiction book on theology, but it was also a social activity. They talked about the ideas in the book but also about how reading the book was affecting their faith. Then they shared a meal together and continued to talk about their lives in a deeper and more personal way. For James, it was a brilliant combination of ideas and relationships.

Abigail put a lot of energy into pleasing people in her community, willing to do whatever she was asked to do. She made meals for every new mother and grieving family and welcomed newcomers to the church. It was frustrating not to be thanked for her efforts. She participated in small groups but found them exhausting. Rather than the group being a place where she could relax and be herself, she felt she needed to be there for others. It didn't feel worth trying to drag her husband there and find a sitter for the kids, but it was the only way to be connected to people in the community.

As a way of stretching herself toward the Pasture, Abigail decided to exercise her agency and volunteer to do something she loved, rather than always doing what she was asked. She remembered how much she had loved helping kids learn to read as part of a college course. So she tried participating in the after-school tutoring program her church partnered with. She made a commitment to stay engaged no matter how little thanks she received. She wanted to do it for the sake of loving others rather than being appreciated. She was able to bring her two younger kids along. Even though they resisted going, she persisted in letting them know this was important to her. After a few weeks, her little boy settled into reading his favorite picture books to kids his own age while her little girl traced letters with some of the younger kids. Even though she didn't receive a lot of appreciation, Abigail felt purposeful and glad to use her gifts in the community.

Practicing Pasture Community

SHARING JOY/GRATITUDE

An essential practice of community for the Pasture is the simple act of sharing gratitude and moments of joy with others. You can start meetings, small groups, potlucks, service projects, and even kids ministry lessons by doing this. This practice not only builds joyful connection, it also primes everyone's nervous system to enter connection mode and decreases the likelihood of people beginning from a place of protection.

CHECKING IN WITH EMOTIONS

We noticed that when we started youth group meetings by checking in on the students' emotions, it benefited both Jungle and Desert dwellers. We gave the students feelings wheels and asked them to choose an emotion word and say one sentence about what they were feeling. For the Jungle dwellers, it helped them sort through their feelings to choose the dominant one and to process how to capture what they wanted to say in one sentence. For the Desert dwellers, it forced them to choose an emotion word (*good* doesn't count) and to offer a few words to personalize the feeling for themselves. Our students grew to love this practice to the point that if we tried to skip it for the sake of time, they would beg to do the check-in. This is an integrative practice for all landscapes because it puts words to emotions and gives a structure to share those emotions in community.

SERVICE OPPORTUNITIES

Jungle dwellers can be drawn to service that is connected to relationships. If these service opportunities bring you joy, by all means, allow Jesus to continue meeting you there. But just as Abigail used her agency, you may need to exercise more choice in serving. That doesn't mean you stop serving; it means you check your motivation. Are you there because you are trying to please someone in particular? Are you expecting intimacy and then feel bitter when you're not appreciated? Are you serving because you feel like you're trying to get someone's attention? Often Jungle dwellers feel they have to serve because their relationships demand it. For a Jungle dweller, the moving practice is to choose to serve because you are sent by Jesus, as one who is loved, to love without expectation of reward. Focus on Jesus' gladness to be with you as you serve rather than on the person you've been trying to please or be noticed by.

Desert dwellers can be drawn to service because it's task oriented and it's the right thing to do. You might prefer to show up at the last minute, do the work, and leave immediately afterward. You appreciate specific tasks and roles. And you are essential for getting things done! Allow yourself to receive Jesus' gladness in your willingness to serve in this way. And as a moving practice, stretch yourself to interact with people more than you might normally. Try something you haven't done before and be willing to ask for help to learn how to do it. Be intentional about affirming other people, thanking them for what they're doing. Ask other people what inspires them to serve. These are ways you can stretch yourself to be more intimate in what have been independent activities for you.

FORGIVENESS/RECONCILIATION

Since Jesus is all about repairing ruptures, forgiveness and reconciliation become instrumental to our understanding of what it means to live in Christian community. After all, we participate with Jesus in his ministry of reconciliation (see 2 Corinthians 5:18-21). It's the ruptures in our relationships that cause us to switch into protection mode and leave connection. We've discussed at length the trouble we get into when we live from a posture of protecting ourselves rather than prioritizing connection. Rather than spending the time here to go into a deep teaching on forgiveness and reconciliation, let's focus on how this practice of community might meet and move both Jungle and Desert dwellers.

Jungle dwellers love the idea of forgiveness because it maintains intimacy and keeps relationships intact. Living at odds with another person can be uncomfortable for a Jungle dweller, and they want to move back into connection. Jesus meets Jungle dwellers in offering forgiveness to each one of us and calling us to practice forgiving sins in community. Jesus also longs for connection to be restored. However, Jungle dwellers tend to rush to forgiveness without being honest about the magnitude of the debt caused by the sin. Jungle dwellers are the ones most likely to say, "It's okay," in response to someone's confession and request for forgiveness. It's *not* okay. But it can be forgiven because Christ forgives us.

Desert dwellers believe in forgiveness because it is the right thing to do in light of Jesus' death and resurrection. We are forgiven, and so the rule is we must forgive others. Jesus meets Desert dwellers in this sense of justice. The only appropriate response to the immeasurable forgiveness we experience from Jesus is to offer forgiveness to others. However, Desert dwellers tend to expect others to ask for their forgiveness but avoid asking others to forgive them. They prefer to overlook the ways they might hurt others because it's too intimate to recognize the ways their sin impacts others. They prefer to avoid the reality that relationships get ruptured and that forgiveness is a necessary first step toward reconciliation. They would rather forget the offense and keep moving. But forgiveness is not forgetfulness. It is a genuine willingness to surrender to Jesus as the debt collector and give up our right to collect what we're owed.[6]

Both Jungle and Desert dwellers will be challenged to practice true reconciliation, the repairing of ruptures. But reconciliation is an essential integrated Pasture practice. It requires mutual ownership of responsibility and genuine trust in God's availability and Jesus' willingness to alleviate all brokenness by taking sin into his own body. Agency is required of all the people involved in reconciliation. There are no passive parties. The offender must exercise agency to make amends and reestablish trust. The offended person must trust in Jesus' presence and the Spirit's work in the other person.

Perhaps no practice is more difficult than forgiveness and reconciliation, especially with enemies.[7] It will never be easy, but when we are deeply attached to God, we can receive Jesus' attunement as he meets us in the hurt we carry. He is available to us. He is in the business of alleviating distress by repairing ruptures, and we can lean into both intimacy and independence as we do the hard work of reconciliation with one another. This is using our agency to love our neighbors as we also love ourselves. None of this is possible from a posture of protection. But from the deep attachment Jesus offers, we can approach reconciliation from our joyful connection with him.

A Church of Confident Faith, Courage, and Connection

The biggest, most comprehensive, most loving, and safest community is found in God the Trinity—Father, Son, and Holy Spirit. Throughout this book we have been dying to talk about the Trinity, but for the sake of clarity, we have focused on Jesus, the Son of God, our Good Shepherd. But so much could be said of our heavenly Father drawing us into a new family. Or the Holy Spirit, through whom we call God our Father and Jesus our Brother. In Jesus, we are drawn into the eternal life and love of the Trinity, and in the community of the Father, Son, and Holy Spirit, our ruptured attachments are repaired.

NEW LIFE–DEEPLY ATTACHED

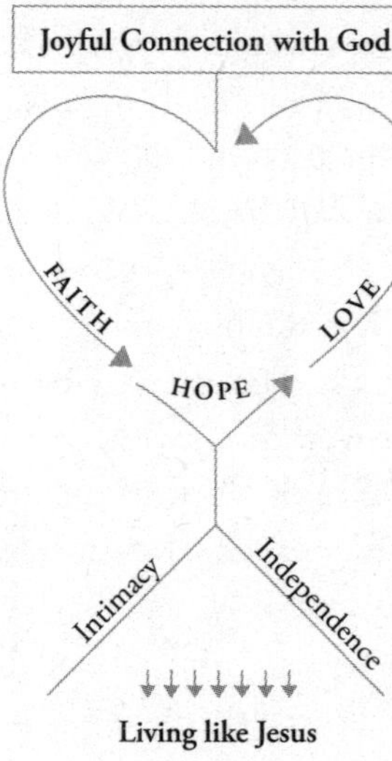

But we are not left just to ponder the invisible, ineffable, and perfect attributes of the Trinity.

God is drawing us into the church. You may not currently be part of a local church for all kinds of reasons. Churches can be hard and painful places. But they can also be breathtakingly beautiful. It is within the church that we are met by our Good Shepherd and moved deeper into the Pasture of Joy and Peace. And it could be no other way. Our distorted defaults and insecure survival strategies can only be healed through ordinary, everyday experiences with other ordinary, everyday people. It is with God's people that we can safely run new experiments of intimacy and independence, gather new information to update our distorted defaults, and practice returning to joy when we blow it.

It is within the church that we experiment with new practices of prayer, Bible reading, worship, and community, discerning when our old attachment strategies are getting the best of us and when what feels hard is really the movement into our life in the Pasture. It is with others that we learn whether we are dragging the Good Shepherd into our insecure landscape or whether he is drawing us into the Pasture. All these things take community.

Throughout part 3 we emphasized how Jesus does three things for us:

- He *models* what it looks like to live deeply attached to God.
- He *meets* us in our survival strategies, offering us care and comfort in our anxious Jungles, avoidant Deserts, and chaotic War Zones.
- And he *moves* us toward the Pasture by giving us the courage and confidence to live a new way.

We need churches to do the same. And we acknowledge that this is a real growth area for most churches.

We need churches full of people who *model* living deeply attached to God. Which means we also need churches full of believers who can *meet* people in their insecure attachment landscapes. And we need churches full of those who help others *move* toward the Pasture with the Good Shepherd. We hope that little by little we can become this kind of people and this kind of church. We invite you to take a step toward this kind of church by responding to the invitation of Jesus to move toward the Pasture and invite a few others to join you. Together we can be a people who are growing into confident faith, courage, and connection.

Acknowledgments

People often say things to us along the lines of "I could never work with my spouse like you guys do!" In response to this, we are often invited to remember that it's only because God has aligned us in our callings that it works so well. So before we acknowledge any people, we notice that none of this would be possible if God hadn't drawn us together and united us in purpose from the very beginning. We don't ever want to take this for granted.

The content of this book has been the center of our work together for the last few years and would not have been as focused without the more than a hundred people who have trusted us enough to sign up for our Attaching to God cohort over the past few years. To each of you, we say thank you for the questions you asked, the stories you shared, and the feedback on how things were landing for you. Your input has been enormous, and we are grateful for your companionship as we continued to refine this material.

We thank Don, our agent, who believed in us and this project from the very beginning; Jillian and Jan, who went to bat for us to acquire this project; and Jonathan, who not only helped us tighten the manuscript but also affirmed the work we were doing in these pages. The art and design team listened to our ideas and came up with beautiful images that dovetail with the content. Thank you to the whole team. You are a publishing house that still cares about God's people more than the bottom dollar.

We've also been surrounded by generous friends who have loaned us houses and cabins in which we have had writing retreats (you know who you are), who have been understanding about our time constraints, and who have asked us how the book is going and encouraged us to continue on.

To our church community at Vineyard Grand Rapids, thank you for your prayers and your friendship, your laughter and your encouragement. You are such good people, and we are glad to be the body of Christ with you.

Notes

PREFACE

1. For the most in-depth and up-to-date statement of attachment theory and theology, see Geoff Holsclaw, "Attachment Theory and Theological Anthropology," https://www.embodiedfaith.life/attachment-theory-and-theological-anthropology.
2. For the most comprehensive introduction to the history and contemporary state of attachment theory and research, looking at the three generations of attachment research, see Robbie Duschinsky, *Cornerstones of Attachment Research* (Oxford University Press, 2020). For the most up-to-date research on attachment and spirituality, see Pehr Granqvist, *Attachment in Religion and Spirituality: A Wider View* (Guilford Press, 2020).

CHAPTER 1: SURVIVING TRAUMA AND HOPING FOR CHANGE

1. Andrew Huberman, *Huberman Lab,* podcast, "Erasing Fears & Traumas Based on the Modern Neuroscience of Fear," December 5, 2021, https://www.hubermanlab.com/episode/erasing-fears-and-traumas-based-on-the-modern-neuroscience-of-fear.
2. Some books will call these *attachment styles*. We are specifically avoiding that language because we don't want you to confuse what we will call *attachment strategies* with personality types.

3. Stephen W. Porges, "Neuroception: A Subconscious System for Detecting Threats and Safety," *Zero to Three* 24 (2004): 19–24. See also Deb Dana, *Anchored: How to Befriend Your Nervous System Using Polyvagal Theory* (Sounds True, 2021).
4. Using "yes, maybe, no" to frame attachment strategies comes from Cindy Hazan and Phillip R. Shaver, "Attachment as an Organizational Framework for Research on Close Relationships," *Psychological Inquiry* 5, no. 1 (1994): 1–22, https://doi.org/10.1207/s15327965 pli0501_1.
5. Anthony Ian Jack, Angela M. Passarelli, and Richard Eleftherios Boyatzis, "When Fixing Problems Kills Personal Development: fMRI Reveals Conflict Between Real and Ideal Selves," *Frontiers in Human Neuroscience* 17 (2023), https://doi.org/10.3389 /fnhum.2023.1128209. Also see Richard Boyatzis, Melvin L. Smith, and Ellen Van Oosten's *Helping People Change: Coaching with Compassion for Lifelong Learning and Growth* (Harvard Business Review Press, 2019).
6. One example is Lindsay Braman's emotion-sensation feelings wheel; see https://lindsaybraman.com/emotion-sensation-feeling-wheel.

CHAPTER 2: ONE DESIRE: JOYFUL CONNECTION

1. James Wilder, "Joy Changes Everything," *Conversations Journal* 12, no. 2 (2014): 47–51. Other resources are Chris M. Coursey, *The Joy Switch: How Your Brain's Secret Circuit Affects Your Relationships—And How You Can Activate It* (Northfield, 2021); and James Wilder et al., *Joy Starts Here: The Transformation Zone* (Life Model Works, 2018).
2. Deb Dana, *Anchored: How to Befriend Your Nervous System Using Polyvagal Theory* (Sounds True, 2021), 41.
3. Louis Cozolino, *The Neuroscience of Human Relationships: Attachment and the Developing Social Brain*, 2nd ed. (Norton, 2014), 162.
4. See Daniel Hill, *Affect Regulation Theory: A Clinical Model* (Norton, 2015).
5. G. G. Coulton, *From St. Francis to Dante* (David Nutt, 1906), 242–243.
6. Wilder et al., *Joy Starts Here*.

7. Allan N. Schore, *Affect Regulation and the Origin of the Self: The Neurobiology of Emotional Development* (Lawrence Erlbaum Associates, 1994), 69–91.
8. Coursey, *The Joy Switch*.
9. See Judith R. Schore and Allan N. Schore, "Modern Attachment Theory: The Central Role of Affect Regulation in Development and Treatment," *Clinical Social Work Journal* 36 (2008): 9–20, https://doi.org/10.1007/s10615-007-0111-7.

CHAPTER 3: TWO DIMENSIONS: INTIMACY AND INDEPENDENCE

1. We want to acknowledge that we are going against the grain of the social psychology stream of attachment research, which labels the two dimensions of attachment through the negative framework of a person being more or less *avoidant* and more or less *anxious* (popularized in the Experiences in Close Relationships questionnaire). We do this for the same reason that Bowlby chose the positive word *attachment* in conscious distinction to his contemporary psychoanalysts, who focused on and labeled pathologies and illnesses instead of health. We will follow Pietromonaco and Barrett, who suggest the positive goals of establishing intimacy and maintaining independence. This also aligns with attachment research that sees attachment as a balance of proximity-seeking and exploration-seeking behaviors. See Paula R. Pietromonaco and Lisa Feldman Barrett, "The Internal Working Models Concept: What Do We Really Know About the Self in Relation to Others?" *Review of General Psychology* 4, no. 2 (2000): 155–175, https://doi.org/10.1037/1089-2680.4.2.155. See also Mary D. Salter Ainsworth and Silvia M. Bell, "Attachment, Exploration, and Separation: Illustrated by the Behavior of One-Year-Olds in a Strange Situation," *Child Development* 41, no. 1 (1970): 49–67, https://doi.org/10.2307/1127388; L. Alan Sroufe and Everett Waters, "Attachment as an Organizational Construct," *Child Development* 48, no. 4 (1977): 1184–1199, https://doi.org/10.2307/1128475; and L. Alan Sroufe, "Attachment and Development: A Prospective, Longitudinal Study from Birth to Adulthood," *Attachment and*

Human Development 7, no. 4 (2005): 349–367, https://doi.org/10.1080/14616730500365928.

2. Rebecca L. Hainlen et al., "Adult Attachment and Well-Being: Dimensions of Differentiation of Self as Mediators," *Contemporary Family Therapy* 38 (2016): 172–183, https://doi.org/10.1007/s10591-015-9359-1.
3. See M. D. Ainsworth, "Attachments Across the Life Span," *Bulletin of the New York Academy of Medicine* 61, no. 9 (1985): 792–812; Jeffrey D. Green and W. Keith Campbell, "Attachment and Exploration in Adults: Chronic and Contextual Accessibility," *Personality and Social Psychology Bulletin* 26, no. 4 (2000): 452–461, https://doi.org/10.1177/0146167200266004; Joseph P. Allen et al., "A Secure Base in Adolescence: Markers of Attachment Security in the Mother-Adolescent Relationship," *Child Development* 74, no. 1 (2003): 292–307, https://doi.org/10.1111/1467-8624.t01-1-00536; and Brooke C. Feeney and Nancy L. Collins, "A New Look at Social Support: A Theoretical Perspective on Thriving Through Relationships," *Personality and Social Psychology Review* 19, no. 2 (2015): 113–147, https://doi.org/10.1177/1088868314544222.
4. We trace these two aspects of the image of God throughout the biblical story in *Does God Really Like Me?: Discovering the God Who Wants to Be with Us* (InterVarsity Press, 2020). For the academic research, see Catherine L. McDowell, *The Image of God in the Garden of Eden: The Creation of Humankind in Genesis 2:5–3:24 in Light of the mīs pî pīt pî and wpt-r Rituals of Mesopotamia and Ancient Egypt* (Eisenbrauns, 2015); and J. Richard Middleton, *The Liberating Image: The Imago Dei in Genesis 1* (Brazos, 2005).
5. The best resource for understanding this balanced approach to cultivating a secure attachment in children is Kent Hoffman, Glen Cooper, and Bert Powell's *Raising a Secure Child: How Circle of Security Parenting Can Help You Nurture Your Child's Attachment, Emotional Resilience, and Freedom to Explore* (Guilford Press, 2017).
6. Daniel J. Siegel developed the idea of a window of tolerance in *The Developing Mind: How Relationships and the Brain Interact to Shape Who We Are*, 2nd ed. (Guilford Press, 2012), 281–286; and Pat

Ogden, Kekuni Minton, and Clare Pain applied it in *Trauma and the Body: A Sensorimotor Approach to Psychotherapy* (Norton, 2006), 26–40.

7. Siegel, *The Developing Mind*, 148.
8. Ed Tronick and Claudia M. Gold, *The Power of Discord: Why the Ups and Downs of Relationships Are the Secret to Building Intimacy, Resilience, and Trust* (Little, Brown Spark, 2020), 39.

CHAPTER 4: THREE DEFAULTS: FAITH, HOPE, LOVE

1. See Mary Main, Nancy Kaplan, and Jude Cassidy, "Security in Infancy, Childhood, and Adulthood: A Move to the Level of Representation," *Monographs of the Society for Research in Child Development* 50, no. 1/2 (1985): 66–104, https://doi.org/10.2307/3333827; and Laura Dewitte, Pehr Granqvist, and Jessie Dezutter, "Meaning Through Attachment: An Integrative Framework," *Psychological Reports* 122, no. 6 (2019): 2242–2265, https://doi.org/10.1177/0033294118799739.
2. The research on internal working models is extensive. For a comprehensive review, see Inge Bretherton and Kristine A. Munholland, "The Internal Working Model Construct in Light of Contemporary Neuroimaging Research" in *Handbook of Attachment: Theory, Research, and Clinical Applications*, ed. Jude Cassidy and Phillip Shaver, 3rd ed. (Guilford Press, 2016), 68. Our particular way of stating this comes from Harriet S. Waters and Everett Waters, "The Attachment Working Models Concept: Among Other Things, We Build Script-Like Representations of Secure Base Experiences," *Attachment & Human Development* 8, no. 3 (2006): 185–197, https://doi.org/10.1080/14616730600856016; and Paula R. Pietromonaco and Lisa Feldman Barrett, "The Internal Working Models Concept: What Do We Really Know About the Self in Relation to Others?," *Review of General Psychology* 4, no. 2 (2000): 155–175, https://doi.org/10.1037/1089-2680.4.2.155.
3. Daniel Hill, *Affect Regulation Theory: A Clinical Model* (Norton, 2015), 112–132.

INTERLUDE: WHERE YOU ARE

1. Faith Hill, "Attachment Style Isn't Destiny," *Atlantic*, February 11, 2023, https://www.theatlantic.com/family/archive/2023/02/attachment-theory-misconceptions-relationship-spectrum/673025/.

CHAPTER 5: JUNGLE GOD: AN ANXIOUS FAITH

1. Daniel J. Siegel and Tina Payne Bryson, *The Power of Showing Up: How Parental Presence Shapes Who Our Kids Become and How Their Brains Get Wired* (Ballantine Books, 2020), 50–55.
2. Amir Levine and Rachel S. F. Heller, *Attached: The New Science of Adult Attachment and How It Can Help You Find—and Keep—Love* (Tarcher Perigee, 2010), 80.
3. The four survival skills we list here for the Jungle are a simplification of the many relational strategies scientifically investigated by Mario Mikulincer and Phillip R. Shaver in "The Attachment Behavioral System in Adulthood: Activation, Psychodynamics, and Interpersonal Processes," *Advances in Experimental Social Psychology* 35 (2003): 53–152, https://doi.org/10.1016/S0065-2601(03)01002-5.
4. Patricia M. Crittenden, "A Dynamic-Maturational Model of Attachment," *Australian and New Zealand Journal of Family Therapy* 27, no. 2 (2006): 105–115, https://doi.org/10.1002/j.1467-8438.2006.tb00704.x.

CHAPTER 6: DESERT GOD: AN AVOIDANT FAITH

1. The four survival skills for the Desert we list here are a simplification of the many relational strategies scientifically investigated by Mario Mikulincer and Phillip R. Shaver in "The Attachment Behavioral System in Adulthood: Activation, Psychodynamics, and Interpersonal Processes," *Advances in Experimental Social Psychology* 35 (2003): 53–152, https://doi.org/10.1016/S0065-2601(03)01002-5.
2. Patricia M. Crittenden, "A Dynamic-Maturational Model of Attachment," *Australian and New Zealand Journal of Family Therapy* 27, no. 2 (2006): 105–115, https://doi.org/10.1002/j.1467-8438.2006.tb00704.x.

3. Iain McGilchrist, *The Master and His Emissary: The Divided Brain and the Making of the Western World* (Yale University Press, 2009), 59.

CHAPTER 7: WAR ZONE GOD

1. Lisa M. Hooper, "Parentification," in *Encyclopedia of Adolescence*, ed. Roger J. R. Levesque (Springer, 2011), published August 12, 2014, 2023–2025, https://doi.org/10.1007/978-1-4419-1695-2_169.
2. Karlen Lyons-Ruth et al., "From Infant Attachment Disorganization to Adult Dissociation: Relational Adaptations or Traumatic Experiences?", *The Psychiatric Clinics of North America* 29, no. 1 (2006): 63–86, https://doi:10.1016/j.psc.2005.10.011.
3. Diane Poole Heller, *The Power of Attachment: How to Create Deep and Lasting Intimate Relationships* (Sounds True, 2019), 114.
4. See Mary Main and Erik Hesse, "Parents' Unresolved Traumatic Experiences Are Related to Infant Disorganized Attachment Status: Is Frightened and/or Frightening Parental Behavior the Linking Mechanism?" in *Attachment in the Preschool Years: Theory, Research, and Intervention*, ed. Mark T. Greenberg, Dante Cicchetti, and E. Mark Cummings (University of Chicago Press, 1990), 161–184; and Robbie Duschinsky, "The Emergence of the Disorganized/Disoriented (D) Attachment Classification, 1979–1982," *History of Psychology* 18, no. 1 (2015): 32–46, https://doi.org/10.1037/a0038524.
5. See Janina Fisher's excellent synthesis of internal parts and trauma therapy in *Healing the Fragmented Selves of Trauma Survivors: Overcoming Internal Self-Alienation* (Routledge, 2017). "Parts" are common to the Jungle and Desert as well, but they are less likely to be as fiercely committed as they are in the War Zone and so do not create as much conflict and chaos as they do in the War Zone.
6. See Jenna Riemersma's excellent *Altogether You: Experiencing Personal and Spiritual Transformation with Internal Family Systems Therapy* (Pivotal Press, 2020).
7. Fisher, *Healing the Fragmented Selves of Trauma Survivors*, 103–125.
8. David J. Wallin, *Attachment in Psychotherapy* (Guilford Press, 2007), 249.

CHAPTER 8: PASTURE GOD

1. The thrival skills are similar to but different from the important relational skills taught by Thrive Today (thrivetoday.org). We are very much in alignment with what Thrive Today teaches and think of them as a valuable resource.
2. We are emphasizing two (vertical and horizontal) integrations of the eight that Daniel J. Siegel discusses in *Mindsight: The New Science of Personal Transformation* (Bantam Books, 2010), 71–75. The other six are the integration of consciousness, memory integration, narrative integration, state integration, interpersonal integration, and temporal integration.
3. See Kathleen Kline, ed., *Authoritative Communities: The Scientific Case for Nurturing the Whole Child* (Springer, 2008) for why we flourish in accountable relationships that are neither authoritarian nor permissive.
4. L. Alan Sroufe, *Emotional Development: The Organization of Emotional Life in the Early Years* (Cambridge University Press, 1997), 172–234.

INTERLUDE: MOVING FROM WHERE YOU ARE

1. See James F. Sorce et al., "Maternal Emotional Signaling: Its Effect on the Visual Cliff Behavior of 1-Year-Olds," *Developmental Psychology* 21, no. 1 (1985): 195–200, https://doi.org/10.1037/0012-1649.21.1.195; and Lynne Zarbatany and Michael E. Lamb, "Social Referencing as a Function of Information Source: Mothers Versus Strangers," *Infant Behavior and Development* 8, no. 1 (1985): 25–33, https://doi.org/10.1016/S0163-6383(85)80014-X.
2. Daniel J. Siegel, *The Developing Mind: How Relationships and the Brain Interact to Shape Who We Are*, 2nd ed. (Guilford Press, 2012), 184–185.
3. This idea of Jesus *meeting* and *moving* us is adapted from research about buffering insecurity and building security. See Lucy L. Hunt, Madoka Kumashiro, and Ximena B. Arriaga, "An Interdependence Analysis of Enhancing Attachment Security" in Laura V. Machia,

Christopher R. Agnew, and Ximena B. Arriaga, eds., *Interdependence, Interaction, and Close Relationships: Advances in Personal Relationships* (Cambridge University Press, 2020), 95–119, https://doi.org/10.1017/9781108645836.006.

CHAPTER 9: BAPTIZED WITH JESUS: ENCOUNTERING JOY

1. Karl D. Lehman, *The Immanuel Approach: For Emotional Healing and for Life* (Immanuel, 2016); and *An Introduction to the Immanuel Approach: For Mental Health Professionals* (Immanuel, 2023).
2. See Karlen Lyons-Ruth et al., "Implicit Relational Knowing: Its Role in Development and Psychoanalytic Treatment," *Journal of Infant Mental Health* 19, no. 3 (1999): 282–289, https://doi.org/10.1002/(SICI)1097-0355(199823)19:3<282::AID-IMHJ3>3.0.CO;2-O; and James L. Fosshage, "The Explicit and Implicit Domains in Psychoanalytic Change," *Psychoanalytic Inquiry* 25, no. 4 (2005): 516–539, https://doi.org/10.2513/s07351690pi2504_7.
3. John T. Cacioppo and William Patrick, *Loneliness: Human Nature and the Need for Social Connection* (Norton, 2008).
4. See Ephesians 1:4-5; Galatians 3:26; 4:4-5; 1 John 3:1; John 1:12, and many more.

CHAPTER 11: TESTED WITH JESUS: FORMING FAITH, HOPE, AND LOVE

1. Recent examples summarize these in the following ways: As the temptations to be relevant, popular, and powerful (Henri J. M. Nouwen, *In the Name of Jesus: Reflections on Christian Leadership* (Crossroad, 1991). As the temptation to focus on security and survival, power and control, or affection and esteem (Thomas Keating, *The Human Condition: Contemplation and Transformation* (Paulist Press, 1999). As the temptation to find our identity in what we can do, what people think of us, or what we have (M. Basil Pennington, *True Self/False Self: Unmasking the Spirit Within* (Crossroad, 2000).

CHAPTER 12: DYING WITH JESUS

1. Amir Levine and Rachel S. F. Heller, *Attached: The New Science of Adult Attachment and How It Can Help You Find—and Keep—Love* (TarcherPerigee, 2010), 153–162. These authors call it the *anxious-avoidant trap*.
2. Richard Beck and Angie McDonald, "Attachment to God: The Attachment to God Inventory, Tests of Working Model Correspondence, and an Exploration of Faith Group Differences," *Journal of Psychology and Theology* 32 no. 2 (2004): 92–103, https://doi.org/10.1177/009164710403200202; Todd W. Hall et al., "Attachment to God and Implicit Spirituality: Clarifying Correspondence and Compensation Models," *Journal of Psychology and Theology* 37, no. 4 (2009): 227–244, https://doi.org/10.1177/009164710903700401; and P. Granqvist, M. Mikulincer, and P. R. Shaver, "Religion as Attachment: Normative Processes and Individual Differences," *Personality and Social Psychology Review* 14, no. 1 (2010): 49–59.
3. For more on discerning through consolation and desolation, see Mark E. Thibodeaux, *God's Voice Within: The Ignatian Way to Discover God's Will* (Loyola Press, 2010).

CHAPTER 13: LIVING WITH JESUS: LOVING GOD, LOVING OTHERS

1. Albert Haase, *Coming Home to Your True Self: Leaving the Emptiness of False Attractions* (InterVarsity Press, 2008), 18–19.
2. See Richard J. Foster's discussion of silence and solitude in *Celebration of Discipline: The Path to Spiritual Growth* (Harper, 1978), 96–109.
3. E. James Wilder et al., *Joyful Journey: Listening to Immanuel* (Presence and Practice, 2020).
4. For an overview of how the themes of God with us and God for us run through the Old Testament as well as the New, see our first book, *Does God Really Like Me?: Discovering the God Who Wants to Be with Us* (InterVarsity, 2020).
5. For more detail on the practice of lectio divina, see Eugene H. Peterson, *Eat This Book: A Conversation in the Art of Spiritual Reading* (Eerdmans, 2006).

6. For an excellent teaching on forgiveness, see Marcus Warner's "Understanding the Wounded Heart—Session 4: Forgiveness," December 1, 2020, by Deeper Walk International, YouTube, 20 min., 33 sec., https://youtu.be/oS59wIGmbUM?si=WbOuReEcpBD2vCUP.
7. For a combination of neuroscience and reconciliation, see Jim Wilder and Ray Woolridge, *Escaping Enemy Mode: How Our Brains Unite or Divide Us* (Northfield, 2022).

About the Authors

Cyd and Geoff Holsclaw are coauthors of *Does God Really Like Me?: Discovering the God Who Wants to Be with Us* and codirectors of the doctor of ministry in spiritual formation and relational neuroscience at Western Theological Seminary. They also cohost the *Attaching to God* podcast and codirect the Center for Embodied Faith (embodiedfaith.life). Cyd is a coach, pastor, and spiritual director, integrating embodied neuroscience and spiritual practices. She teaches spiritual direction at Friends University. Dr. Geoff Holsclaw is a visiting professor of theology at Western Theological Seminary.